Solving the People Problem

SOLVING

THE

PEOPLE PROBLEM

Essential Skills You Need To

——— ***Lead and Succeed*** ———

In Today's Workplace

BRETT M. COOPER AND EVANS KERRIGAN

LIONCREST
PUBLISHING

SOLVING THE PEOPLE PROBLEM

Essential Skills You Need to Lead and Succeed in Today's Workplace

ISBN   978-1-5445-0836-8 *Hardcover*

       978-1-5445-0835-1 *Paperback*

       978-1-5445-0813-9 *Ebook*

To my lovely wife and best friend, Joan, who has taught me to honor our differences, making our lives together so much richer.

—EVANS

To Sophia and Olivia—May the ideas in this book help you solve all the people problems you encounter in life.

—DAD (A.K.A. BRETT)

CONTENTS

INTRODUCTION

Few in her organization were surprised when Sierra received her big promotion into a position of leadership. She was an intelligent, hardworking high achiever. She was good with people, and in her recent stint as acting supervisor, she had been able to consistently motivate her team to go above and beyond expectations.

When she formally stepped into her new position, though, Sierra found herself, for the first time in her career, feeling poorly equipped for the challenges ahead. Much to her surprise, she discovered that the old skills that had raised her to this position didn't fully prepare her for her new leadership role. Her extensive knowledge and adeptness with the technical side of her work provided her with few strategies to improve her communication, motivation, or support for her team.

As her former sense of being "part of the team" dissipated, she began to see that the "team" wasn't a single, organized unit with a single perspective. It was a group of individuals, each of whom had their own needs and priorities.

Bill was extremely social and enthusiastic. He thrived on conversation and generating ideas at a blazing pace. Robert was the opposite. When he did speak up, his ideas were always precise and articulate, but he often spent the whole meeting in silence, anxious to get back to some solitude and independent work time.

Mary fell somewhere between the two. Like Bill, she was always happy to support her fellow team members and was quick to point out when others had done great work. However, like Robert, she was quiet in meetings. Too often, she was simply unwilling to give her opinion on the topic at hand.

Each of these team members had years of experience and had proven time and again their value in their respective positions. They all had advanced degrees and were considered experts in their specialized areas. Each of them spoke English as well as other languages. Yet, it seemed to Sierra that whenever they were in the room together, none of them were able to understand what the others were saying.

Everyone had their own set ways of tackling their responsibilities, and each way was different from how Sierra approached her work. She was strong-willed, self-assured, and hyperfocused on getting things done quickly. She believed that success depends on building momentum. Yet, these same factors that had inspired her success didn't seem to matter to anyone on her team.

Sierra needed this group of individuals to come together *as a team*, but she struggled to find the right language to make that happen. She couldn't expect Bill, Robert, and Mary to work together, share ideas, or cut through the rising level of frustration until she could help them explain why they felt uncomfortable with how the team currently communicated.

She knew there was a problem in how her team related to one another, but she couldn't quite say what it was or how to solve it.

Do any of these issues sound familiar?

Sierra's story isn't uncommon. Moving into a position of leadership is often a shock. Many of us, when we get that big promotion to a supervisory or management position, don't know what to expect next. Before being promoted into a leadership position, many of us focused on being the best individual contributor we could be. Now we're required to not only manage ourselves but also to understand how others think and feel. We have to be able to encourage everyone to make the most meaningful contributions. Our new job is as much about creating a space for people to work comfortably and efficiently as it is about the technical know-how that got us the job in the first place.

Whether you are just starting your leadership journey or you've been a leader for years, your future success will largely be determined by how well you work with people and how well you inspire them to work with you.

THE PEOPLE PROBLEM

Leading effectively can be difficult for the experienced manager as well as the newcomer. Often, those who have spent decades in leadership positions still struggle to communicate effectively and inspire others across their organization.

Consider James Patrick, who runs his own IT firm. Over the years, his leadership choices led to a serious delegation problem.

James struggled with the people side of his job. Communication wasn't his strength. He felt most comfortable tackling the technical side of his work. Because of this personality preference, his team leaders would bring him technical problems to solve that really should have stayed off his desk.

Instead of sending those problems back to his team, James

decided that assisting with these issues would allow him to show his commitment and support without stepping out of his communication comfort zone.

In the end, no one was served well by this arrangement. Senior members of James's team were passing off their responsibilities to such an extent that James lacked the time to attend to more strategic issues. Those in supporting roles were confused about whether to make their own decisions or to ask James for direction on their tasks.

In short, James's office was dealing with some major dysfunction.

No one created this dysfunction on purpose, but with his willingness to take on the technical tasks for his own comfort, James was largely to blame. Managers who reported to James thought he preferred to remain directly involved in every problem. James thought he was making a positive contribution to the work environment. While there were clear problems with this arrangement, no one quite knew how to address them or even how to start a conversation about them.

In both Sierra's and James's situations, the problem wasn't lack of technical knowledge or experience. The problem was people: how to talk to them, how to encourage them, how to organize them, and how to empower them.

The people problem is present in every workplace, and it is a hard one to solve alone. This is true no matter how you came into your position of leadership or how long you've been in it.

Maybe you're the senior executive who would be more productive if you delegated more. Maybe you're the newly promoted supervisor who has to influence the technical specialists to work together more productively. Maybe you're a team leader who wants to better manage all the differing points of view on your team.

No matter your industry, your position, or your experience, your struggles come down to the same people problems:

- How do I make decisions that positively influence everyone?
- How do I ensure that people understand what I am trying to communicate?
- How do I steer conflict and disagreement in a positive direction?
- How do I encourage everyone on the team to speak up and share ideas?

In a nutshell: How do I get this group of vastly different individuals to work as a team and succeed?

FINDING THE FRAMEWORK TO MAKE IT WORK

There are many complexities woven into our work relationships. The solutions to both the simple and the difficult issues, however, often come from a novel place: our emotions.

The modern work environment is in desperate need of emotional intelligence, which, as *Psychology Today*[1] puts it, is "the ability to identify and manage one's own emotions, as well as the emotions of others." Workers in America today spend as much as 85 percent of their working hours interacting with their peers.[2] They go to meetings together, flesh out strategies over the phone, and send updates over email. Their work is the work of compromise, camaraderie, and communication.

And yet, the skills that would enhance their ability to communicate and work together are often glossed over by their organization and their leaders. Instead, businesses implement new systems and hardware in the pursuit of increased productivity. But by neglecting to work on communication and team skills, they continue to suboptimize their results.

Developing emotional intelligence in the workplace out-

---

1   "Emotional Intelligence," *Psychology Today*, https://www.psychologytoday.com/us/basics/emotional-intelligence.

2   Rob Cross and Scott Taylor, "How to Manage Collaborative Overload," *Babson Thought & Action*, January 30, 2018, http://entrepreneurship.babson.edu/manage-collaborative-overload/.

weighs most other skill development options. In one study by TalentSmart, it was found to account for 58 percent of job success.[3] It is urgently needed in almost every position in every industry. And it doesn't get the attention it deserves. Daniel Goleman, one of the pioneers in the field of emotional intelligence, analyzed the competency models used by major organizations and categorized those competencies into technical skills, IQ, and emotional intelligence. He found that emotional intelligence was shown to be twice as important a driver of outstanding performance as either of the other categories.[4] This held true across a broad range of job positions and became even more important for success as leaders moved into higher levels of responsibility inside the organization.

If you can learn to harness your emotional intelligence enough to understand how and why you behave as you do—and how and why others behave as they do—you can adjust your actions and reactions to create the space for understanding and success.

Your decision-making process, your communication style, and your approach to team management, conflict, and leadership are exactly that: yours and yours alone. They

3   Travis Bradberry, "Why You Need Emotional Intelligence to Succeed," *Inc.*, March 12, 2015, https://www.inc.com/travis-bradberry/why-you-need-emotional-intelligence-to-succeed.html.

4   Daniel Goleman, "What Makes a Leader," *Harvard Business Review* (January 2004), https://hbr.org/2004/01/what-makes-a-leader.

are your tendencies and preferences. Effective leadership means knowing yourself, connecting with people who have their own styles, and building a relationship that honors those differences.

But how do you learn—and how do you teach—emotional intelligence? To do that, you need a framework that explains how people behave and why they behave that way. It has to provide an effective solution to your people problems that works on an emotional and practical level.

That framework is precisely what you'll learn in this book.

Together, we'll walk through the incredible insights of DISC-EQ, a synthesis of psychologically based models developed by some of the foremost experts in the field. DISC-EQ will tell us the how and why of our behavior and the behavior of others, while providing concrete steps we can employ to bridge differences.

Long before you reach the last page, you'll see that the gaps between you and your colleagues are not as vast as you think.

Using the information and direction in this book, you will become more emotionally intelligent. You will become more aware of your own personality preferences and be able to adapt your approach to communicate more effectively with others, allowing you to create the high-quality, efficient, positive work environment your team and organization want and need.

FACING THE RELATIONSHIP CRISIS IN THE WORKPLACE

Businesses are failing to address the relationship crisis occurring in their workplaces. Business leaders are ever more frequently trying to use technical solutions to solve their people problems. They look to data analysis, AI, and specialized apps, but the solutions to the biggest hurdles they face won't be found on a screen. Solving the people problem is rooted in building emotionally authentic interactions.

Emotional intelligence is a challenge in today's world partly because our genuine, trust-filled work relationships are disappearing. Increasingly, we communicate via those same screens, instead of through person-to-person conversation. We build our relationships through texts, Facebook, Instagram, email, and other apps. All of us joke about people sitting together and "talking" through their instant messages instead of engaging in a personal dialogue. How often are we one of the characters in this scene? In the work environment, we put more thought and time into our spreadsheets and reports than in how we communicate with our colleagues.

We look to technology to improve our efficiency, but only true people connection creates the environment we need to get the work done. It's been proven that a happier worker with strong, positive work relationships is a more productive employee.[5] Our technological tools can create efficiency in our communications, but that speed and simplicity has a price. We need real human connection to make those interactions effective.

This is all the more crucial because we live in the era of team-based creative work. Gone are the days when most people worked in isolation on individual tasks. Teams working on complex projects have become the standard across the whole economy. These days, communication and good relationships are of central importance, and yet, these factors are consistently pushed aside.

That's the discovery we made a few years into our partnership. For almost ten years, we helped organizations implement process improvement efforts using Lean Six Sigma. Those projects generated hundreds of millions of dollars in savings for our clients. Yet, we could see that we—and the organizations we were serving—were missing something. We eliminated process inefficiencies and streamlined work procedures, but we came to realize we were not getting to the heart of the real problem these organizations were facing. Because the heart, we discov-

---

5   Cross and Taylor, "How to Manage Collaborative Overload."

ered, was the problem. Humans are social and emotional creatures by nature, and companies and organizational development efforts have been ignoring that fact for far too long.

The best and brightest in business know this already. In an article from the World Economic Forum,[6] a group of international senior executives were asked to predict the most important skills of tomorrow. Their answers were not a list of technical abilities. Instead, these leaders focused on an increase in what many call soft skills, such as empathy, teamwork, and resilience. In other words, it's emotion and our ability to work together that matters in the workplace these days.

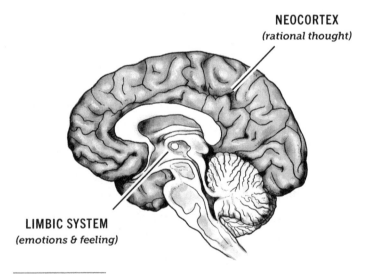

NEOCORTEX
(rational thought)

LIMBIC SYSTEM
(emotions & feeling)

6   Stéphanie Thomson, "The Most Important Skills of Tomorrow According to Five Global Leaders," *World Economic Forum*, October 14, 2016, https://www.weforum.org/agenda/2016/10/the-most-important-skills-of-tomorrow-according-to-five-global-leaders.

Science backs this up. Neuroscientific studies have shown that our limbic system (the emotional segment of our brain) reacts more quickly than our neocortex (the rational part of our brain).[7] This system is in charge of the fight-or-flight response, and it was very helpful in the prehistoric hunter-gatherer era, when a false move might mean death in the jaws of a predator. Fortunately, we don't face such threats very often in the modern world. Unfortunately, this portion of the brain has not kept up with societal evolution. Today, when emotions get fired up, they shut down the rational thinking that helps us regulate our responses, just as they did fifty thousand years ago. We can react just as quickly to an offhand comment in a meeting as we would to a charging saber-toothed tiger. It's the same fight-or-flight response, only it's moved from the cave to the conference room.

Thanks to our physiological wiring, many of the issues that get in our way when working together are more emotional than rational. It's the emotional limbic system hijacking the rational neocortex that causes many of the challenges we struggle with on teams and throughout the workplace. That's where we have to look to fix what's broken.

Many of the major performance issues organizations face these days revolve around this lack of emotional intelligence. Put simply, people just don't know how to

---

7   Jennifer Delgado, "Emotional Hijacking: What Happens to Your Brain When You Lose Control?" *Psychology Spot*, https://psychology-spot.com/emotional-hijacking-what-happens-to/.

communicate and work together effectively. They don't know how to accommodate different personalities and get the best out of everyone. In many cases, they are not even aware of how their own thoughts and personality traits contribute to the problems they are experiencing.

This is the issue around which we founded our company, Integris. We've worked with organizations of every size in many different industries, and we've seen the toll that this emotional dysfunction can have on even the best of them. It shows up in every kind of organization, from government agencies, to midsize private companies, to the largest of multinationals.

If you want people you work with to succeed, thrive, and produce great results, you've got to create an environment where they can contribute and bring their best to the challenges at hand. That means addressing them as individuals, each with their own personality and set of preferences and talents. It is critical to meet their emotional needs as well as their rational ones.

THE SOLUTION STARTS WITH YOU

You are not doomed to live in a workplace filled with dissatisfied workers trudging through the day filled with impersonal relationships. No organization or leader has to be resigned to emotional coldness, hurtful conflict, and poor communication.

You can create an emotionally positive, efficient work environment, but to do so, you'll have to be the one to lead the way.

Emotionally healthy organizations start with, and are driven by, emotionally healthy leaders. So you have to take the lead on becoming a more emotionally intelligent leader who is able to understand different perspectives. You have to become aware of your personality style, comfort zones, and limitations. Then you have to learn to read the needs and preferences of others and consider those differences when making decisions and communicating, be it one-on-one or with a group. You need to understand what's happening under the surface with people in order to help resolve unproductive, emotionally fueled conflict and inspire people to work together.

Your team isn't likely to make this happen without you. As leadership gurus Jim Kouzes and Barry Posner write in their best seller, *The Leadership Challenge*,[8] "Leaders go first." And in this case, that means you.

That's how Sierra resolved the tension in her team. It's how James resolved his delegation difficulties.

We've seen it happen a thousand times across dozens of

---

8   Jim Kouzes and Barry Posner, *The Leadership Challenge: How to Make Extraordinary Things Happen in Organizations*, 6th ed. (Hoboken, NJ: Wiley, 2017).

industries in our twenty years together. With the tools in this book, you can solve the people problem, too. You can be the change agent to increase the health of your team, but it has to start with you.

We wrote *Solving the People Problem* to share powerful ideas and insights for improving communication, teamwork, and organizational culture. These lessons are helpful no matter your role or current organizational environment. After all, the people problem exists everywhere.

However, this book is not a manual for how to fix other people. It's a guide to improving relationships through a framework that tells us *why* there's a problem and *how* to solve it.

If you commit to doing this work yourself—to leading, whether you hold a formal leadership position or not—we will show you the way forward to a more productive work environment that's also more satisfying, more honest, and more fulfilling for you and everyone around you.

With a little self-awareness and a commitment to making critical changes in your work relationships, you can reduce or eliminate the frustration caused by clashes in personalities. Instead, you can leverage those differences to create new possibilities for your team.

It all starts with you. And it all starts here.

PART I

THE FOUNDATIONS OF EMOTIONAL INTELLIGENCE

---- *Chapter 1* ----

KNOWING YOURSELF TO KNOW OTHERS

On paper, the two of us should never be able to work together productively. Our personality styles are simply too different.

Evans is reflective, cautious, and introverted. Brett is more of a fast-paced extrovert with a higher tolerance for risk.

At the end of a long day of presenting or working with clients, Evans likes to head back to the hotel room for a quiet evening on his own, while Brett likes to meet up with friends and colleagues to chat late into the night.

These preferences don't just come up in our personal time; they also affect how we work and how we work together. In meetings, Evans is more accommodating. He speaks up less often and may set aside his ideas and concerns (unless they are particularly strongly held positions) in order to keep things running smoothly. Brett, on the other hand, is far more assertive with his ideas. He makes sure to find a way to share his thoughts, even if that means the meeting will go long.

In our professional interactions, Brett is a "talk it through" leader, and Evans is a "think it through" leader.

The potential hazards in our work relationship are obvious. It's easy to imagine the two of us struggling to work effectively together on a project, let alone founding and running a successful company. Reading over the contrasts in our styles, you might assume that every meeting would involve Brett pushing all of his ideas and Evans quietly accommodating him. In that scenario, Brett might feel like he was doing all the heavy lifting, and Evans might feel like his opinions were never considered.

It could go that way, but it doesn't. The reason is, we have learned to *see the differences* and *honor the differences* between us.

We recognize how we are different, and we strive to find ways to honor and capitalize on those differences to make our partnership—and our organization—stronger.

Evans recognizes his temptation to walk away from impassioned discussions where he really should speak up. So he tries to be assertive enough to voice his thoughts. It's very easy for Brett's enthusiasm to shut others out of a conversation. So he tries to slow down, stop talking, and encourage others to contribute.

Most importantly, we recognize that neither of our personality styles is better than the other. In fact, we know we're stronger because we bring our styles together. Brett likes to verbalize and discuss ideas in the moment, and Evans prefers to think through ideas on his own before presenting them to the group. There are benefits to both of these preferences, so long as we create the space to accommodate and lift up each other.

On your team, you *want* different perspectives and different styles. That's what allows you to find the best solutions and implement the best strategies. The trick is learning to *see the difference* and *honor the difference* in each person so everyone feels comfortable bringing their best to the team and making their most valuable contributions.

DISCOVERING THE DIFFERENCE WITH JOAN

Even those of us who are usually attentive to the differences that exist between individuals may still fail to notice those differences when we aren't paying close attention.

Such was the case with Evans's wife, Joan, and her work on our team with Brett. Joan is a graphic artist who has led design projects for Integris over the years. Early on, though, significant tension arose between her and Brett—tension caused by the people problem.

Because he's a talk-it-through leader, Brett would continually build on previous conversations with Joan regarding her projects. He would regularly offer new suggestions for tweaks and incremental changes. To him, working through the gray area in this way was an effective and dynamic approach to the creative process. Knowing that Joan was a creative type herself, he erroneously assumed that she enjoyed ideating in the same way.

Joan, on the other hand, saw things as more black or white. She didn't recognize that Brett was just being vocal with ideas as a means of collaboration. Instead, she thought every idea variation was a request from him for a finished design. As such, she'd put in several hours to "get it just right," only to have Brett see—and suggest—new opportunities for additional modifications.

The process made Joan exceptionally frustrated, but it took time for Brett to learn this. You see, Joan is also very quiet and reserved, so she did not let Brett know how uncomfortable this was making her.

This people problem could have been largely avoided if Brett and Joan had been more attentive to and more communicative about their preferences. When they finally discussed their individual approaches to the creative process, they were able to quickly come to an understanding about how to work best together.

Today, Brett and Joan are able to cocreate together effectively, largely because they understand each other. Brett strives to make it clear when he's looking for a draft mock-up versus a final product. Joan double-checks before putting in the extra work required to get something "perfectly right." Both err on the side of caution by overcommunicating their questions, comments, and concerns.

KNOW YOURSELF

Brett and Joan had to be proactive in how they solved their people problem. The tension between them wasn't due to any lack of interest on either part. They had simply been blind to what was going on beneath the surface in their interactions.

To some extent, we're all ignorant of our biases and how those biases affect others. We can make every effort to be friendly and accommodating, but that doesn't mean others see us in that light. Nor does it mean we understand the behaviors of others with any clarity.

In a study reported in the *Harvard Business Review*, researchers measured the self-awareness of five thousand people and found that the majority (95 percent) considered themselves highly self-aware. Ironically, the researchers found that despite people's *belief* in their own self-awareness, only 10 to 15 percent of them actually met the study's criteria for possessing true self-awareness, such as having a clear picture of their emotions, accurately recognizing how they react to situations, and how they were viewed by others.[9]

The gap between our biased view of ourselves and how others actually see us goes a long way toward explaining why the people problem is so entrenched in the workplace. It also explains why building healthy relationships in your organization has to start with self-awareness.

This has been true since the dawn of philosophy. One of the most famous quotes attributed to Socrates, the founder of the Western philosophical tradition, states simply, "Know thyself."[10] Two millennia later, Leonardo da Vinci echoed the same point, saying, "One can have no smaller or greater mastery than mastery of oneself."

In the twentieth century, one of the founders of modern

---

9   Tasha Eurich, "What Self-Awareness Really Is (and How to Cultivate It)," *Harvard Business Review*, January 4, 2018, https://hbr.org/2018/01/what-self-awareness-really-is-and-how-to-cultivate-it.

10   "Know thyself" is an ancient Greek aphorism with uncertain origin. While the source of its first usage is unknown, Plato and others attributed it to Socrates in their writings.

psychology, Carl Jung, agreed, adding, "Your visions will become clear only when you can look into your own heart."

From ancient Greek philosophy to contemporary psychology, the ability to understand and overcome our limitations has started with introspection, and for good reason. We have to be able to recognize the motivations arising within us before we can begin to make the necessary changes that address our strained work relationships. Awareness has to start with us, otherwise we struggle, as Brett and Joan did, to even perceive the problem.

When we observe others, we run their behavior through our own lens of priorities and biases. We make assumptions about their reasoning, their intentions, their feelings about us, and much else based on our interpretation of their actions. Putting ourselves in their place, we think, "If I had done that, I would have done it for *this* reason."

These assumptions are often very far removed from the actual motivations that drove the other person to act that way.

Had Brett lacked the insights found within this book, he might have seen Joan as being purposefully uncommunicative or stubborn. He might have assumed she didn't like him or didn't want to work with him.

To resolve this difference, Brett had to be mindful of how

his personal style influenced how he approached the creative process with Joan. Only when he could see that *his* way of developing content was not *Joan's* way was he able to step back, reexamine their interactions, and create a process that worked better *for both of them.*

Simply recognizing that difference and finding a way to honor it has allowed Brett and Joan to work together successfully for years now.

Knowing yourself is critical to building positive relationships at work. We know this beyond philosophy and anecdote. Research conducted at Washington University, Rutgers University, and the University of California[11] found that having greater clarity about yourself correlates to being better able to understand the experiences of others. In other words, when we make introspection a priority, we're stronger, more flexible, and better able to empathize and connect with others.

THE FUTILITY OF POINTING FINGERS

We've all seen office disagreements that grow into major problems over something as simple as a poorly worded email. Hit "Send" too soon, and we can soon be looking

---

11 Nathaniel S. Eckland et al., "A Multi-Method Investigation of the Association between Emotional Clarity and Empathy," *Emotion* 18, no. 5 (August 2018): 638–645.

at huge misunderstandings and massive amounts of emotional friction.

Of course, it's not just email. Whenever we communicate—as the sender or receiver of information—we share or see only part of the picture. Because of this, two parallel but different conversations take place between the individuals involved, especially when emotions are running high. If we can pause long enough for the two angry parties to explain their motivations and perspectives, we'll often find that the issue was not in the original intent of the words but in the fact that no one had a clear understanding of the whole picture.

These realizations are only possible when we suspend the urge to point fingers. Whenever we're part of a disagreement or misunderstanding, we all have an urge to insist, "I'm right!" The implication, of course, is that everyone else is wrong.

When we point fingers, we ascribe blame. We also shut ourselves off from introspection. We look at the situation from only our own perspective.

In such moments, we leave no room to honor or even appreciate the differences. Yet, it is only through asking questions, listening, and making an effort to better understand one another that we can discover resolution. Most workplace disagreements cannot and should not be reduced to "I'm right; you're wrong." They usually involve two or more people with unique, valid perspectives.

Therefore, to resolve these disagreements, we have to be willing to challenge the stories we tell ourselves about our own thoughts and behavior and the thoughts and behaviors of others.

With Brett and Joan, Brett assumed that all creative people liked to talk things through and make changes throughout the creative process. Joan assumed Brett was purposefully being critical of her work by making so many suggestions. Neither person meant harm to the other, but if they had decided to point fingers instead of examining their assumptions, they never would have found a way to honor their differences and create a work relationship that has become very successful.

WE ALL BRING STRENGTHS; WE ALL BRING LIMITATIONS

We feel a natural bias for our own perspective. It's very easy to get trapped in an "I'm right" approach to every interaction. When we are good—even great—at what we do, we often struggle to see when our strengths suddenly turn and become our limitations.

For example, decisiveness can be a real asset for a leader,

but only so long as the best ideas are incorporated into their decisions. Likewise, skepticism is critical in reviewing new data and discussing new ideas, but skepticism becomes a limitation if it becomes dismissive of *all* new data and *all* new ideas.

Any personality trait can be a strength or a limitation, and any person can use their traits to strengthen or limit their team.

The best leaders know this, so they strive to assemble teams with a large set of diverse perspectives. For a team to be successful, we need colleagues with different approaches and different ideas to not just be present but also actively involved in conversations and decisions. After all, if we could do it on our own, why have a team at all?

Teams thrive when members share and discuss the personal priorities that influence their perspective. Some people prioritize data, detail, and perfection, while others put more focus on big-picture thinking and creating enthusiasm. Some people prioritize quick decisions and progress, while others prefer to take extra time to collaborate and be sure everyone is on board before moving ahead.

None of those preferences is fundamentally better than the others. In fact, all of them are incomplete. Each preference introduces important strengths into a team, which, when overused, can also weaken a team. There are times when any of these preferences may provide the answer for the problem at hand. For that reason, real success requires us to assemble a team that can value and appreciate the full range of perspectives.

INSIGHTS: BRETT'S IDEATING

We periodically use a powerful exercise with our team that we call "The Appreciation Seat." We gather the team around a table and take turns letting each person sit in the Appreciation Seat. When you are in the seat, you start by hearing an accolade from each of your colleagues—something you do that really helps the team. After all have given an accolade, we go around the room a second time so people can share a potential improvement opportunity—something you do that slows down the team or impedes progress.

During one of Brett's sessions in the Appreciation Seat, one of our colleagues, Renee, started by telling Brett, "The thing you do that really pushes us forward is your ideating. You're always thinking about the future. You're always thinking about what's next for us."

As we worked around the circle and returned to Renee,

she said to Brett, "You know, the thing you do that slows us down is your ideating." Everyone laughed out loud, including Brett, because we all knew exactly what she meant. Renee continued, "While the rest of us are working to execute on an idea—often one you initiated—you are already onto the next big thing. That can draw focus away from the team's ability to successfully implement projects."

Renee was pointing out a common scenario: when overused, a person's greatest strength can become a limitation. This bit of feedback has stayed with Brett for years, giving him a valuable reminder of the danger of overplaying his strength as a visionary. Thanks to this one simple exercise, Brett gained an insightful piece of knowledge that made him a better leader and made us a better team.

THEY DON'T TEACH THIS ENOUGH TO LEADERS

The two of us are not new to business. We have between us more than fifty years of experience in sales, management, and consulting. We both earned MBA degrees. So we can confidently say that professional training courses and school programs, in general, don't have a great record teaching these skills. More companies and schools are now realizing the impact and have added these topics to their curriculum but not all and not enough.

To this day, we still hear from employers that the biggest skill gaps they see in their employees are interpersonal, not technical. Much of that comes down to the priorities of their educational institutions. MBA classes teach us about finance, marketing, IT, and strategy—a whole host of useful technical skills—yet, they have little to say about what we should do when we work with people whose views we don't understand and whose methods seem completely foreign to us.

In business, rarely do colleagues stand around the water cooler and discuss their biases, instincts, and perceptions. For most, talking about personal priorities and communication preferences isn't a natural thing to do. Although there's no doubt in the power of such conversations, the fact is that they tend to happen only when someone makes a conscious effort to bring it up.

Successful relationships are the key to running a successful business. To build those successful relationships, you need enough self-awareness to recognize your strengths and when your strengths are becoming your limitations—when you are bringing the team together and when you are causing fissures in the team's sense of camaraderie.

We all have different styles, and we need to be able to *see the differences* and *honor the differences* between everyone in the workplace (and outside of it, for that matter). There are billions of people on this planet and as much variety as there are individuals. Our job as leaders is to find a way to activate all of those talented, unique individuals around us. To do that, we need a comprehensive model that can help us understand ourselves and others.

Chapter 2

THE SOLUTION, PART I

RAISING YOUR EMOTIONAL INTELLIGENCE

Not every relationship has a happy ending. Even those who have reached the pinnacle of leadership can struggle to maintain strong interpersonal connections with colleagues who have extremely different personality styles.

Such was the case with Jack, the CEO of a prominent medical organization. Jack is an incredibly social guy. If you like a good conversation, you'll always get one with him.

As a person who cares deeply about his relationships with his fellow workers, you might assume Jack would run a very amiable workplace. This was generally true in his office, except in the case of his CFO, Lauren. Lauren's approach to relationships ran counter to Jack's. While she cared as deeply as Jack about her work relationships, she saw lengthy chatting sessions as a waste of time during work hours. Like Joan in the previous chapter, she preferred to focus on data and the details of the task at hand.

These two highly successful individuals simply couldn't comprehend each other. From Jack's perspective, Lauren was rejecting his friendship and camaraderie by refusing to sit down and chat. It seemed to him that all she cared about was getting to the meeting, arguing over every point, proving she was right, and leaving.

That wasn't how Lauren saw it. She saw herself playing a key role on the team: the person who challenges assumptions to strengthen every idea. She showed how much she cared by how hard she worked. So she struggled with the loose way Jack transitioned between important business topics and chitchat.

Lauren thrived on clearly defined expectations and direct communication that related to the task at hand. From her perspective, Jack seemed to be insisting that she waste time when she could be focusing on what was important. By linking business meetings with friendly conversation, she felt he was discouraging her attempts to challenge the ideas in the room and limiting her contribution to the team.

For four years, this relationship continued to sour without

the tension ever being addressed. Even though they knew there were issues, they lacked a language and structure to deal with the differences.

When Jack and Lauren finally began investigating each other's perspective using the tools we cover in this book, they both gained greater awareness. Jack discovered that while his strength was in supporting people and building relationships, Lauren's reticence in this area was not a sign of disagreeableness, just a different personality style. Lauren, meanwhile, came to understand that Jack wasn't putting conversation and "palling around" above the work at hand; he saw collaboration as a crucial part *of the work.*

For the first time, both could see that they cared equally about the job and their colleagues. Both were working hard in the way that made sense to them.

In the case of Jack and Lauren, that insight came too late. The history of intense disagreements they had over time was a big hill to climb toward reconciliation. Repairing a relationship takes more than awareness; it takes a willingness to act—to move away from our comfort zone and reach out to the other person. By the time they understood the problem, neither Jack nor Lauren was able to build that bridge toward reconciliation.

Neither Jack nor Lauren wanted it to come to this. They had

hoped that becoming aware of each other's motivations would be enough to salvage their working relationship. In the end, even though they were able to see their differences, they couldn't find a way to honor those differences, at least not with each other. And so, Lauren decided to leave the organization for another opportunity.

DISC-EQ: PUTTING A NAME ON EMPATHY

If Jack and Lauren had discovered DISC-EQ earlier in their careers—before the conflict got out of hand—they could have avoided all the harm and pain caused by their assumptions and hurt feelings. For every Jack and Lauren, we've encountered countless examples of people who have been able to repair their relationships. The lesson of this story isn't that you can't overcome a damaged work relationship but that you have to start working on it now and take action immediately.

You can frame that action around DISC-EQ, a framework built off two well-established psychological models: DISC and EQ. We're going to cover the DISC part of this framework in the next chapter. Here, we're going to discuss just what EQ means and why it is crucial to the success of our work relationships.

INSIGHTS: A NEW SYNTHESIS

It is important to note that the underlying models in this book are not our own creation. DISC-EQ is a synthesis of two well-established concepts—"DISC" (the language of personality style) and "EQ," or emotional intelligence (the understanding of the emotional side of human interaction). DISC-EQ is not a new DISC assessment but rather a new perspective on how the concepts and language of DISC language can be used to effectively and directly build higher levels of emotional intelligence.

For years, these two frameworks have been used independently by leaders, teams, and organizations around the world with impressive results. Now, for the first time, we have combined these ideas to provide leaders like you with even more powerful advice and guidance. Now you can solve the people problem by increasing your DISC-EQ and building workplace relationships that really work.

EQ is shorthand for the term "emotional intelligence," and we will use the terms interchangeably in this book. The letters stand for emotional quotient, which is often seen as the counterbalance to IQ (your intelligence quotient). However, there are some crucial differences between the two. First, your EQ doesn't come with a set number like IQ (which is complicated and controversial in its own right). Second, many people assume EQ is as fixed and unchangeable as IQ, and that simply isn't true.

IQ is largely genetic, and most of us stay within a certain, small range our whole lives. EQ, on the other hand, is undeniably malleable. You can increase your EQ simply by reading this book and putting the insights to work.

EQ is the collection of skills and insights within us that allow us to better manage ourselves and to create strong, positive relationships with others.

The identification of these skills can be traced back to thinkers such as Socrates, but the more concrete ideas behind emotional intelligence are only a few decades old. In 1996, Daniel Goleman published a book called, fittingly, *Emotional Intelligence*. In it, he took the term "emotional intelligence"—which had been coined by Peter Salovey and John Mayer in 1990—fleshed it out, and popularized it.

In *Emotional Intelligence*, Goleman states that EQ counts for a lot more than IQ or technical skills when it comes to predicting who is going to be successful in the workplace. Success, Goleman suggests, is largely determined by a person's ability to interact with others in an effective way. We are, as humans, social creatures. For those who struggle to be effective socially, life—and life at work in particular—is going to be more difficult.

Two decades after Goleman's seminal book, Travis Bradberry and Jean Greaves published *Emotional Intelligence 2.0*, where they simplified and further clarified Goleman's concept into four elements of emotional intelligence—Self-Awareness, Self-Management, Social-Awareness, and Relationship Management.

Since the work of Goleman, and Bradberry and Greaves, additional research has continued to back up the critical importance of emotional intelligence. For instance, in a recent LinkedIn Workplace Learning Report, managers, executives, and trainers all ranked emotional intelligence skills as the highest priority when developing talent in their organizations. They valued the ability to collaborate, communicate, and lead far more highly than the technical skills most assume are the keys to success.[12]

As ongoing research further proves the truth behind the concepts outlined by Goleman, and Bradberry and Greaves, the real-world applications of emotional intelligence continue to evolve. In this book, we take emotional intelligence to the next level by demonstrating a practical

---

12   Josh Bersin, "LinkedIn 2019 Talent Trends: Soft Skills, Transparency and Trust," *LinkedIn*, January 29, 2019, https://www.linkedin.com/pulse/linkedin-2019-talent-trends-soft-skills-transparency-trust-bersin/.

and proven approach for quickly and effectively developing the essential EQ skills you need to lead and succeed in today's workforce.

We've placed all of these ideas into a framework we call DISC-EQ. Within the simple two-by-two matrix below lies all the insights you need to transform all your work relationships.

	AWARENESS	APPLICATION
SELF	*Know Your Style*	*Choose Actions Wisely*
OTHERS	*Know Other Styles*	*Adapt Behavior for Mutual Benefit*

The DISC-EQ Framework

With this framework, Jack and Lauren—and all the rest of us—can explore our own motivations and actions, recognize how others are responding to those actions, and decide how we can adjust those actions to improve our relationships.

EXPANDING AWARENESS

We know that everyone is different, but most of us don't put much thought into how that difference manifests in our work experience. We have to broaden our awareness of ourselves and others by looking more closely at how we perceive and interact with the world and how others might perceive and interact with us.

To reach those insights, you need to both know your own style as well as the styles of others.

KNOW YOUR OWN STYLE

Knowing your own style is the basic understanding of your thoughts, actions, and behaviors. To break it down a little further, self-awareness is an awareness of your *internal* motivations and your *external* behavior. For simplicity, we call these motivations and behaviors your style.

You may think the need for introspection is a little obvious, but a lot of people, when they act, don't examine the drivers behind their actions. They just move forward.

The lack of self-awareness in the workplace is more common than you may think. In a survey conducted with 467 working adults across multiple industries in the United States, almost everyone reported working with at least one person who "displayed a complete lack of insight into how they were coming across." Making matters worse, half of the people surveyed claimed to work with at least four such people.[13]

---

13   Tasha Eurich, "Working with People Who Aren't Self-Aware," *Harvard Business Review*, October 19, 2018, https://hbr.org/2018/10/working-with-people-who-arent-self-aware.

Most people don't stop to think about their style traits, such as why they always want to be in charge during meetings, or always need to be so critical of ideas, or always need to be right, or always want to be the center of attention. They simply act on their impulses. This sets them on a collision course with those who approach things differently.

To really understand why you do what you do, you need to discover your priorities. Priorities are what you value highest in your interactions with the world. In a work environment, do you take the time to cultivate relationships, or do you focus your attention on working with data and project content? Do you have a tendency to skip what you see as "minor details" in an effort to get something done quickly, or do you prefer to go slowly and get it precisely right the first time?

In short, what are your primary motivations? What makes you tick?

There is no right or wrong answer to these questions, but there are different answers. To make any major progress in creating a healthier work environment, you have to understand *your* answers so you can see how they shape *your* behavior.

Take, for instance, someone who answered the above questions by saying they focus on data and working slowly and precisely. They are likely motivated by things such as stability and accuracy.

This person isn't going to promote a shoot-from-the-hip strategy in meetings. They might not speak up as much during brainstorming sessions. They almost certainly aren't going to stick around afterward to build those personal relationships with their teammates when they could instead be working on other tasks.

Another person in that room might answer those questions by saying they value collaboration and see their relationships with others in the room, not as a distraction, but as the very means of attaining results. Further, they might like to move fast, viewing perfection as something that gets in the way of action.

This person will probably be more willing to change course on a project, so long as that means things keep moving ahead in a positive direction. They'll likely speak up more during brainstorming because it is important to them that all their ideas are heard. They may be glad to stay and chitchat after the meeting, viewing personal connection as a key element of a productive work environment.

How do these two people perceive the actions of each other?

Very quickly, we can see why so many coworkers struggle with frustration and misunderstanding when working together.

KNOWING OTHER STYLES

Samantha is our director of operations here at Integris. As with any new member of the team, when she first came on board, Brett was very conscientious about making her feel comfortable and welcome. As you've probably picked up by now, Brett prefers more active and energetic work and finds mundane and repetitive tasks mentally draining. So, in his attempt to help Samantha feel engaged and enthusiastic about her new company, he made every effort to keep what he thought was "busy work" off her desk. However, he made the mistake of projecting *his own* priorities onto Samantha. As it turns out, Samantha enjoys the solitude of those tasks. In fact, she welcomes taking them off the plates of others on the team who do not.

This scenario highlights why knowing your own style isn't enough. Once Brett learned more about Samantha's style preferences, he was able to draw upon his awareness of those around him and recognize that Samantha was craving the exact work he was withholding.

Sometimes insightful, empathetic people can have excellent self-awareness and still fall short in their efforts to communicate effectively with others. Brett meant to communicate a sense of welcome and comfort to Samantha, but he did so by concentrating on what his self-awareness told him *he* would want to experience on *his* first days.

Avoiding these mistakes requires something beyond just personal introspection. It requires a keen awareness of how others see and interact with the world. Once you use introspection to figure out who you are and what makes you tick, you can build on those revelations to see more clearly *how* others are different from you. That insight allows you to sneak a glimpse at *why* others act the way they do, without imprinting your own motivations onto their behavior.

Whether it's Brett and Samantha or Jack and Lauren, we can already see that much of the turmoil we experience in the workplace isn't about bad actors acting badly but basic misunderstandings built on false assumptions. This reality is at the core of the people problem. And recognizing this fact is our first, powerful step toward more positive work relationships built upon DISC-EQ.

Becoming aware of how others perceive and interact with the world, however, takes work. Think of the last time you were driving and someone abruptly cut you off. What was your reaction?

You might have been quick to think the other driver was a horrible person—that they were selfish, reckless, thoughtless, and dangerous. You may have responded by honking, swearing at them in your head, or doing something more dramatic and observable.

But what if you found out that the person was on the way to the hospital after getting a call that someone they love had been hurt? Or what if you learned they were late for a flight because an important business meeting had run long?

If you knew there was a worthwhile underlying reason for why they cut you off, how would that change your reaction? Would you draw different conclusions about the type of person they are? Might you even pull over and give them room to pass?

This is the power rooted in expanding your awareness of how other people are wired. When you realize that your colleague is asking for more data because they care about accuracy, you might change the narrative you've been telling yourself that they are just difficult to work with. When you recognize that your coworker who seemingly dominates meetings is just a talk-it-through kind of person who needs to verbalize their ideas to gain clarity, you might become less frustrated that they never stop talking.

Other people's motivations and priorities are not worse than our own; they're simply different. Becoming socially aware is about recognizing that. It involves slowing down enough to not only see someone's actions but also to try to actually understand their actions *from their perspective.*

Some people are driven by results. Some people are driven by their enthusiasm. Some people are driven by their relationships. And some people are driven by their ability to complete their tasks perfectly.

In order to create a healthy and effective workplace, all of these priorities are necessary. To make them work together, we have to recognize those style differences for what they are, and we have to honor them. We must look beyond our own biases and recognize that others are seeing the same situation in a completely different light.

APPLYING YOUR AWARENESS

The model shown above has one column for "Awareness" and another for "Application" to highlight what we already know from Jack and Lauren's story: awareness of different styles doesn't, in and of itself, resolve personal conflicts or create effective relationships. For Jack and Lauren, they simply couldn't move beyond awareness. Taking action was a step further than they were able to go with each other.

Strengthening our awareness is merely the first step toward building healthy, productive relationships. Actively applying that awareness is what actually enables relationships to improve. This comes with both a focus on the self—in choosing your actions wisely—and with a focus toward others—in adapting your behavior for mutual success.

CHOOSE YOUR ACTIONS WISELY

As you become more conscious of your own style tendencies, it becomes possible for you to apply that awareness to make better, more productive choices in a range of situations.

For example, Evans's natural style is to be collaborative and supportive of others. He has no problem with allowing others to take the lead. However, in our work, there are many times when Evans is tasked with delivering quick results. In such circumstances, where there simply is no time to let things play out in a more measured pace, Evans tells himself that his typical approach might end up being a limitation. So he stretches outside of his normal comfort zone to make quicker, more independent decisions. It's not his first choice in how to act, but because he has a great deal of self-awareness, he knows it's the *right choice* in how to act, given the needs of the situation.

In scenarios like the one above, Evans's *knowledge* of his tendency to let things unfold is necessary but inadequate on its own. To be more effective, he needs to apply that knowledge as he chooses which actions to take. For all of us, when we challenge our own thinking and ask ourselves,

"Am I approaching this in the best way possible for this situation?" we are much more likely to choose actions that result in positive and productive outcomes.

ADAPT YOUR BEHAVIOR FOR MUTUAL SUCCESS

In many cases, you will be able to choose your actions wisely independent of the styles of the people around you. But as a leader in the workplace, very frequently it will be the styles of the people around you that dictate the best response.

Consider the following scenarios and ask yourself if having more clarity about the tendencies and priorities of the other people involved would influence you to adjust your behavior:

- You want to recognize your teammate for a job well done, and you don't know if they appreciate public recognition or if they prefer a quiet thank-you behind closed doors.
- You are going in to talk with your boss about an important project, and you don't know if she cares more about the big picture or the minute details.
- You are in an important meeting with your team when tensions start to rise, and you don't know how to motivate each person to stay engaged and voice their opinions.
- You are heading to lunch with an important customer,

and you don't know if they prioritize the personal relationship with you or the quality of your products.

In each of these situations, you would be able to make a more productive decision about what actions to take if you knew the styles of the other people.

- Publicly recognizing a teammate who hates public recognition is not an effective way to say thank you.
- Going into a meeting with your boss with pages and pages of spreadsheets when all she wants to know is whether the project will be done on time is not likely to go well.
- Using the same technique to appeal to different people with different priorities is not likely to get the group back on track.
- Spending the lunch hour asking about your customer's family is not likely to close the sale if your customer wants to know all the technical specs of your products.

By building your awareness of other people's individual styles and by using that knowledge to adapt how you behave, you stand the best chance of navigating difficult situations and building work relationships that are productive and mutually successful.

WHERE DO YOU STAND? TAKE THE DISC-EQ SURVEY AND FIND OUT!

To solve the people problem, you must increase your awareness of yourself and others, and you must apply your emotional intelligence to choose your actions wisely and to adapt your behavior for mutual benefit. We've designed the rest of this book to help you achieve those goals. But do you know where you currently stand?

For almost twenty years, we have been helping people, teams, and organizations plan and implement change initiatives. One thing we know to be true for any change effort is that starting with an accurate measure of your current state is crucial to your success.

If you wanted to lose weight, would you start a diet and exercise program without knowing your current weight? If you wanted to run a faster mile, would you start a training regimen without knowing your current time? Of course not.

To find out your current state of DISC-EQ, pause your reading and go online to take our DISC-EQ Survey. Your personalized DISC-EQ Report will be available immediately, giving you powerful insights that will help as you read the rest of this book. Just go to SolvingThePeopleProblem. com, click the "What's My DISC-EQ?" link and enter the code STPP-BK to launch your complimentary survey (most people complete it in five to ten minutes).

FROM CONCEPT TO LANGUAGE

Welcome back! What did you learn? Did you see yourself exhibiting some of these skills and behaviors more frequently than others? Do some of the actions seem to happen naturally, while others feel a bit more foreign?

No matter your results, there's always room to improve. And doing so is at the heart of solving the people problem.

These are skills that can be learned. You just need a tool—a language—that will help you better understand your own style traits and priorities as well as the natural characteristics of those around you. In other words, you need DISC.

Chapter 3

THE SOLUTION, PART II

DISC: THE LANGUAGE OF PERSONALITY

Long before he'd ever heard of DISC-EQ, Jack was well aware of the personality problems in his office—how could he not be? In fact, he'd gone down the personality assessment path before, and it hadn't been very helpful.

His organization had tried another instrument in the past. Jack felt the results were somewhat accurate—and personally very interesting—but most team members couldn't remember how all the different personality types related to one another. Some even struggled to remember the acronym of their own type.

It took some time before Jack could believe that DISC would be different. When he and his team finally agreed to give it a try, they found much more value in DISC. DISC provided accuracy, a focus on the practical side of personality, and the ability to help improve communication and relationships across a wide range of situations. It was far simpler to understand and to act upon.

By learning the DISC vocabulary of personality, Jack could begin to understand the motivations of the people in his office in relation to the four DISC styles—Dominance, Influence, Steadiness, and Conscientiousness. Jack could finally put into words why his I-personality that craved enthusiasm and strong relationships was constantly in a state of conflict with Lauren's quiet, detail-oriented C-personality. He could also explain other tensions in the office by looking at the behavioral tendencies of those who were more assertive (D-personalities) or were more accommodating (S-personalities).

The EQ insights of the last chapter made Jack and his team aware of the people problem in the office. Now they needed a way to talk about those differences. They liked the ideas that were brought up in the EQ discussion, but they needed a tool that could help them identify and increase their awareness of styles and help apply that knowledge to the real world. In order to assess and manage their differences effectively, they needed a language that allowed them to communicate with one another more precisely. Relationships require communication, and communication requires language. When it comes to our preferences, motivations, and behaviors, the best language we've found is DISC.

Expanding his EQ had been mind-opening for Jack, but it was DISC that provided him with the concrete explanations he needed to fully understand that people approached relationships in a different way than he did. As we saw in the last chapter, DISC-EQ didn't save Jack's relationship with Lauren, but the insights gained from it were still very useful. They improved the outlook of the team and the productivity of the whole office.

A LANGUAGE FOR EQ

Much of what we discussed in the last chapter—the core concepts of emotional intelligence—might seem like common sense. And, to some extent, they are. However, as Mark Twain is often credited with saying, "Common sense is the least common of the senses." While it might be fairly straightforward to *recognize* the importance of being aware and applying that awareness to our relationships, that's really just the *what* of emotional intelligence. The challenge for most of us is the *how*. And that's where the DISC part of DISC-EQ comes in.

DISC provides us with a language about personality—as well as a visual guide—to explain how our varied personalities interact with one another. With DISC, we can immediately see why contrasting preferences and motivations lead to vastly different decisions and behaviors.

The need for an EQ language can't be underestimated. For years, linguists have recognized that the languages we speak influence how we think and what we think about.[14] Studies have shown that when we don't have the words to describe a phenomenon, we often can't even see it.

Take colors. Linguists have found that people who speak languages with more words for various colors can actually *see* more colors because of that more extensive vocabulary. For instance, those who are bilingual in English and Greek may recognize more shades of blue than those who speak English alone, simply because the Greek language uses multiple words for the color.[15]

Similarly, in a study reported in the *Journal of Experimental Psychology*, the same researcher, Professor Panos Athanasopoulos, concluded that "by learning a new language, you suddenly become attuned to perceptual dimensions that you weren't aware of before." Their findings support "a

---

14 Guy Deutscher, "Does Your Language Shape How You Think?" *The New York Times Magazine*, August 26, 2010, https://www.nytimes.com/2010/08/29/magazine/29language-t. html?pagewanted=all.

15 Panos Athanasopoulos, "Cognitive Representation of Color in Bilinguals: The Case of Greek Blues," abstract, *Bilingualism: Language and Cognition* 12, no. 1 (January 2009), https://www.cambridge.org/core/journals/bilingualism-language-and-cognition/ article/cognitive-representation-of-colour-in-bilinguals-the-case-of-greek-blues/ B1B1CA4B7C8D9618365D9C59454DE2DA.

growing body of evidence demonstrating the ease with which language can creep into our most basic senses, including our emotions, our visual perception, and our sense of time."[16]

Over the course of our work with thousands of teams and individuals, we've seen many people become more attuned to the elements of emotional intelligence after learning the language of DISC. Having that language helps people perceive realities they simply might not have been able to see before. Beyond *perception*, the language of DISC also makes it much easier to *communicate* around these concepts. After all, even if we could identify the various dimensions of emotional intelligence through intuition without the aid of words, how would we communicate those insights to others?

Imagine you went on a journey to China, and you couldn't speak or read the language. Although you may be incredibly eager to engage with the culture and the people who live there, it would be almost impossible to do so on any deep level without a shared vocabulary from which to work. You wouldn't be able to read the signs or ask anyone for directions. You wouldn't even be able to ask for their names.

---

16 Panos Athanasopoulos and Emanuel Byland, "The Whorfian Time Warp: Representing Duration through the Language Hourglass," *Journal of Experimental Psychology: General* 146, no. 7 (2017): 911–916.

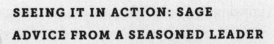

SEEING IT IN ACTION: SAGE ADVICE FROM A SEASONED LEADER

I have seven direct reports, each with a DISC style that is different than mine, and my primary responsibility as a leader is to support them so they can be professionally and personally successful in our organization. By increasing my DISC-EQ, I've learned to understand what my colleagues need from me and how I can communicate more effectively with them, both as individuals and as an intact team.

My advice to other leaders? Be proactive about building your own emotional intelligence as well as the emotional intelligence of those around you. Start by learning the language of DISC, then bring it to life by actively discussing expectations and communication preferences with your team.

GARY, CEO

LEARNING THE LANGUAGE

One of the great benefits of DISC is that the language is incredibly simple to understand. As mentioned above, DISC starts by placing all personalities into a set of four broad categories: **D**ominance, **I**nfluence, **S**teadiness, and **C**onscientiousness.

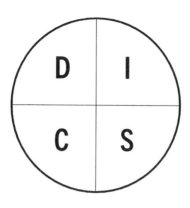

Those whose personalities fall into the D style are often outspoken and results focused. They make sure their voices are heard in meetings and that something is accomplished by the time those meetings end. I-personalities like Jack are usually very relationship focused. They're enthusiastic, friendly, upbeat, and talkative, which is why Jack's meetings always ended in a long chat.

An S-personality is usually on the quieter side. Very friendly like their I-style colleagues, they are warm, accepting, and concerned for how everyone is doing. If someone is having a hard day, an S-personality will be there with a shoulder to lean on. C-personalities, on the other hand, tend to keep to themselves. They are often the critical thinkers in an office. They may not always be the life of the party, but when you want a complicated project done right, you can usually go to them.

That is just the broad-strokes overview—a relatively simple

and straightforward "first look." We're going to get into some of the nuance of DISC in a bit. For now, though, this basic, easy-to-follow framework is one of the key benefits that separates DISC from many of the other tools that attempt to explain personality-style differences.

INSIGHTS: FROM THE MIND THAT CREATED WONDER WOMAN

The ideas expressed in DISC have a long history. The ancient Greek physician Hippocrates identified people by four temperaments. Fast forward to the early twentieth century, and we see similar ideas incubating in the minds of figures such as Sigmund Freud and Carl Jung.

The DISC framework itself first appears in 1928, coming from a surprising source: William Moulton Marston, the man who would go on to create the comic book character Wonder Woman. Marston was an incredibly interesting man. A trained psychologist, he not only developed the model for DISC and one of the world's most powerful superheroes, but he also helped create the lie detector.

So insightful was Marston that his foundational work on DISC still forms the basis for today's most advanced personality assessments. The terms associated with each personality type have evolved—his choices were seen as a little too judgmental and not as descriptive as the ones we've laid out above—but the core theory has remained largely unchanged over the last century.

ESTIMATING YOUR PRIMARY DISC STYLE

"Primary" style references the four quadrants of the wheel: D, I, S, and C. On a very general level, we can determine your primary DISC style with just two basic questions:

- Do you consider yourself more questioning and skeptical or more accepting and warm?

More questioning and skeptical   More accepting and warm

- Do you consider yourself more fast-paced and outspoken or more cautious and reflective?

More fast-paced
and outspoken

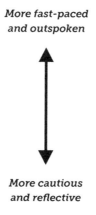

More cautious
and reflective

Obviously, most of us aren't just one of those choices or the other entirely. We may be outspoken in some moments and reflective in others. For the purposes of this exercise, though, make a judgment about yourself and which way you act most typically.

Once you have your answers, we can now place you in one of the four primary DISC styles.

STEP 1: Questioning and Skeptical OR Accepting and Warm?

- If you consider yourself more questioning and skeptical, you will fall to the left half of the DISC wheel. This would put you as either a D or C style.
- If you consider yourself more accepting and warm, you will fall to the right half of the DISC wheel. This would put you as either an I or S style.

STEP 2: Fast-Paced and Outspoken OR Cautious and Reflective?

- If you consider yourself more fast-paced and outspoken, you will fall to the upper half of the DISC wheel. This would put you as either a D or I style.
- If you consider yourself more cautious and reflective, you will fall to the lower half of the DISC wheel. This would put you as either a C or S style.

STEP 3: Estimate Your Primary Style

- By combining your answers from steps 1 and 2, you'll be able to estimate which quadrant is your likely primary style—D, I, S, or C.

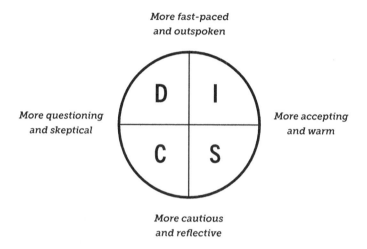

- D: Fast-paced and outspoken; questioning and skeptical
- I: Fast-paced and outspoken; accepting and warm
- S: Cautious and reflective; accepting and warm
- C: Cautious and reflective; questioning and skeptical

A QUICK LOOK AT THE FOUR PRIMARY STYLES

Now that you've estimated your primary style, let's take a look at some common personality traits to see if your style estimate feels right.

- If you estimated yourself to have a D style, we'd expect you to have some of these traits:
  - Self-confident
  - Direct
  - Decisive
  - Ambitious
  - Comfortable with taking risks
- If you estimated yourself to have an I style, we'd expect you to have some of these traits:
  - Enthusiastic
  - Charming
  - Sociable
  - Optimistic
  - Persuasive
- If you estimated yourself to have an S style, we'd expect you to have some of these traits:
  - Patient
  - Cooperative
  - Calm
  - Good listener
  - Humble
- If you estimated yourself to have a C style, we'd expect you to have some of these traits:
  - Precise
  - Analytical
  - Systematic
  - Reserved
  - Quiet

If at least three of the five traits apply to you, we'd say we got it about right. If two or fewer apply, we suggest you go back to steps 1 and 2 and reconsider your answers. It is quite possible that you are "in the middle" on one or both of the questions, which would make the estimation process less precise.

SEEING IT IN ACTION: THE AHA MOMENT

We have a diverse employee population, with a wide range of different personality styles. As part of our "Creating a High-Performing Organization" initiative, we decided to focus on emotional intelligence by building a unified vocabulary around DISC.

What I love to see is that aha moment when teammates begin to talk about their DISC-style differences, especially their individual propensities to be either more questioning and skeptical or more accepting and warm. In what seems like the blink of an eye, people start to recognize all the things they've historically misunderstood about their peers. Past frustrations and disagreements are examined in a new light, and team productivity skyrockets almost immediately.

SARAH, VICE PRESIDENT OF CHANGE LEADERSHIP

THE COMMON MOTIVATORS AND STRESSORS BEHIND THE LETTERS

With just this very quick style estimate, we can already tell a lot about ourselves and others. For example, let's take a look at situations and scenarios that tend to be motivating or stressful for people with different styles. When you get to the section about your style, read closely and decide if some (or even all) of these ring true for you.

- People with D-personalities tend to be motivated by:
  - Achieving results
  - Working toward challenging goals
  - Taking action and getting things moving
  - Making decisions
- Stressors for Ds usually include:
  - Following strict rules and protocols
  - Being forced to pay attention to the emotional needs of others
  - Slowing down to accommodate others
- I-personalities, in contrast, are often motivated by the following:
  - Creating enthusiasm
  - Taking action and getting people involved
  - Collaborating with others and developing warm relationships
  - Being outgoing and sharing ideas freely
- Their major stressors in the workplace might be:
  - Giving people unpleasant feedback

- Being isolated for long periods of time
- Performing routine tasks that lack excitement

Moving to the cautious and reflective side of the DISC wheel (the lower half), we see some similarities between Is and Ss in their motivators and stressors.

- Those S motivators might include:
  - Supporting people when they face a challenge
  - Collaborating with people who genuinely care about each other
  - Contributing to a calm and stable environment
  - Being helpful and accommodating the needs of others
- Their stressors could relate to any of the following:
  - Working in a chaotic environment without clear guidelines
  - Giving people negative feedback
  - Having to speak up and argue for their point of view

Cs share much of the skepticism of Ds and the cautiousness of Ss.

- The motivators that energize their work might include:
  - Emphasizing accuracy and precision
  - Challenging inefficient systems or procedures
  - Working in a stable environment where chaos and uncertainly don't threaten the quality of their work

- ◦ Being an expert
- At the same time, they are far more likely to find situations like these stressful:
  - ◦ Being wrong or unprepared
  - ◦ Being forced to mingle with strangers
  - ◦ Making quick decisions without time for analysis

How closely did you connect with the motivators and stressors we listed? Did a good number of them align with what you know to be true about yourself? In our experience, while each and every motivator or stressor listed may not apply equally to every person who has the same primary D, I, S, or C personality style, we find that even at this general level, estimated styles are valid guidelines to help us better understand how we and others process our work and the world around us.

INSIGHTS: SHOULD YOU COMPLETE A DISC ASSESSMENT?

We wrote this book to be a stand-alone guide for using DISC to expand your emotional intelligence and improve your relationships. To get the most out of this book, you naturally need to have a good sense of what DISC style you have, which is why we included the estimation process above. But the estimation process is simply that—a quick and easy way to get an idea of where you fall on the DISC wheel.

There are a number of tools on the market designed to give you a more accurate reading of your DISC style. Even though all these products are certainly not created equal (which makes sense given that they can range from free to costing several hundreds of dollars), we absolutely believe in the value of using online DISC assessments. Here are two reasons you might choose to take an online assessment to augment what you learn from this book:

- To get a more precise identification of your DISC style. Rather than asking just two questions—as we did earlier in this book—online assessments can use a large data bank of questions, all designed to pinpoint your style. In fact, the most robust assessments use what's called computerized adaptive testing, which allows the assessment to really narrow in on your tendencies and preferences. The result is a personalized report that is more accurate than the fixed-list survey alternatives.
- To receive tailored advice based on your assessment results. Throughout this book, we provide a lot of valuable advice. Some of the online assessment tools offer reports that get even more detailed in their guidance, which they can do because they have a more accurate and reliable reading of your style.

WHERE YOUR AUTHORS FALL ON THE DISC MODEL

Based on the information we've shared about ourselves, can you guess where we fall on the DISC wheel? Brett is more outgoing and energetic. Evans is more reserved and focused on supporting others. Both of us value collaboration and maintaining positive relationships.

Where would you put us?

If you guessed Brett is an I, you'd be right. He's an enthusiastic leader who likes to take quick action and collaborate with others. Evans, on the other hand, is an S. Like most S-personalities, he loves to support others, maintain some stability, and collaborate with the team.

We are, of course, much more than just the sum of these characteristics. But if you were going to work with either of us, knowing our DISC traits would give you a sense of how to communicate with us more effectively.

For example, if you were a team member presenting a project plan to Brett, you might highlight how your ideas will push our organization forward and get people excited and engaged. And in sharing your ideas with Evans, you might emphasize aspects of how your plan will support people through the change.

In both cases, you'd be presenting the same overall plan. But by knowing what energizes each of us as individuals, you would be better equipped to share your ideas in a way that is most likely to meet each of our unique needs and thus ensure your message is heard. This scenario showcases the power of DISC as a roadmap for navigating relationships and engaging in effective communication.

INSIGHTS: DISC VS. DISC

Before we go further, we want to explain a subtle difference in how the term "DISC" can be written. In this book, we mostly write it with all capital letters—as DISC. However, there will be times you'll see it written with a lowercase *i*—DiSC. Although this might seem like the most minor of distinctions, the difference in capitalization is significant, and addressing it here will help avoid confusion as you continue your DISC-EQ journey beyond the pages of this book.

DISC (all capitals) is the psychological theory developed first by Marston in the 1920s. DiSC (with the lowercase *i*)—or more officially, Everything DiSC®[17]—is an extensive suite of validated assessments and products based on the core DISC concept. Everything DiSC® includes a

---

17   Everything DiSC® © by John Wiley & Sons, Inc. Everything DiSC® is a registered trademark of John Wiley & Sons. All rights reserved. Permission granted by John Wiley & Sons.

foundational assessment called Workplace, along with specialty assessments for applications such as management, sales, teamwork, and handling conflict.

In full disclosure, we use Everything DiSC® in our work at Integris because we find the assessments to be highly accurate and reliable and the personalized reports to be robust and insightful.

However, this book isn't a sales pitch for Everything DiSC®. It's a guide for using the DISC framework to increase your emotional intelligence and create healthier work environments, regardless of whether you are using Everything DiSC®. To this end, for the duration of the book, we will use the DISC abbreviation.

THE RISK OF MISREADING DISC

DISC is very much about creating positive, fulfilling, and thriving relationships between ourselves and those we work with. However, DISC can only provide effective advice when we understand what the styles mean and what they can and cannot tell us about ourselves and others.

Before we move on to all the amazing ways that increasing DISC-EQ can improve your leadership and your work relationships, we should spend a moment looking at the risks of misreading DISC.

NEITHER POSITIVE NOR NEGATIVE

We often encounter people who feel disappointed by where they land on the DISC wheel. That disappointment isn't due to an inaccuracy in the DISC model. It comes from the preconceived biases a person carries into the process. For example, some think only Ds can be leaders or only Is can be salespeople. This is simply not true.

"I was really hoping to be a D," they might say. Or, "I'd rather be an S."

It's understandable that we want to see certain qualities within ourselves, and sometimes our lack of self-awareness can be a little surprising. However, in truth, some of this disappointment is a misreading of what DISC is.

We've said it before, and we will continue to say it: there is no better or worse DISC style. Each comes with its own strengths and limitations.

D-personalities are not necessarily destined to be leaders. Even when they are in leadership positions, they can create a positive influence or a negative one, depending on how they manage themselves. Every DISC personality style can lead and contribute to their team and organization. Success for the individual and the team comes down to how each person uses their innate skills and talents.

If not properly understood, DISC can seem limiting. Is and Ss establish good relationships with others. Ds and Cs are critical thinkers. Ds and Is take action. Cs and Ss create stability in the workplace. By that reductive logic, an S would never be a leader, and a D could never empathize with a colleague. An I would fail to take account of the facts, and a C could never be energetic about change.

This simplistic notion of DISC is very much a misreading of the framework. Any personality type can be an effective leader. And, in truth, we are all a blend of styles to some degree. All people care about relationships, clear thinking, and making progress toward their goals. They just approach these scenarios and goals *differently*. They place a different priority on them, which drives them to act in different ways.

This is where EQ really makes a difference. High emotional intelligence allows us to recognize these different approaches. It also allows us to see whether we are leveraging the inherent strengths of our style or falling prey to the common limitations associated with it. For example, Ds with low emotional intelligence often exhibit the worst of the D style. They don't come across as assertive or decisive. Instead, they're seen as aggressive and insensitive. They don't seem bold but, rather, bossy and confrontational.

Meanwhile, an I with low EQ may come across as easily

distracted and impulsive instead of warm, engaging, and persuasive.

An S on the low end might seem passive and indecisive, completely counter to a highly emotionally intelligent S, who appears to others as patient, supportive, and a good listener.

Cs can range from appearing critical and defensive on the low end to thorough, systematic, and meticulous on the high end.

Wherever you fall on the DISC wheel, you can be an effective leader. There is no good or bad—or better or worse—style. We all have a comfort zone. To be as effective as possible, we all need to be able to maximize our strengths within that comfort zone while remaining adaptable to the needs of others.

YOU STILL NEED TO GET TO KNOW PEOPLE

DISC can tell us a great deal about ourselves and others, but it isn't an excuse to avoid getting to know people. We have to resist any temptation to stereotype people and assume we understand the full depth of their personality and experience based solely on what we know about their DISC style. It is important to remember that every person is unique. DISC simply gives us a language to work with so we increase the depth of our understanding and improve our emotional intelligence.

As we've seen, the DISC framework can capture a lot of nuance, but it could never provide a complete portrait of a living individual. We encourage using DISC to pinpoint where conflict or misunderstanding might arise with others, not as a means to label others.

A person with an I-personality shouldn't be put into a box in which all she represents is her enthusiasm, nor should a C-personality be reduced to "just a critical thinker." People are complex beings, and DISC style, while being an important aspect, is just one piece of the puzzle. Upbringing, training, and personal experiences all contribute to making us who we are.

DISC is only effective when we utilize it to enhance our understanding and interactions. The insights it provides are powerful and invaluable, but they are also not meant to be applied in a vacuum.

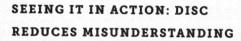

SEEING IT IN ACTION: DISC
REDUCES MISUNDERSTANDING

As a new leader in my organization, I was getting to know all the people I would be working with in my twenty-five-person group. Most of those I talked to warned me of one particular member of our team: Jerome, an employee with over twenty years' experience in his role. Most of the team felt Jerome was too negative. He was pessimistic and always looking for a reason that a task could not be done. For my part, I had been put into this position because of my ability to make things happen, and it sounded like Jerome would represent a big challenge.

Luckily, at that moment, the group was taking DISC assessments. Thanks to DISC, Jerome and I had a language to investigate our differences and see how we could honor them. We discovered that I was an outgoing, results-driven D, whereas Jerome wasn't a pessimistic naysayer; he was just a strong C-personality. He was extremely conscientious and skeptical, and he needed a lot of data before he could get on board with the team's ideas.

Jerome and I actually found a way to capitalize on these differences. I began bringing my ideas to him before I introduced them to the group as a whole. Jerome's skep-

tical nature provided me insights into where my ideas were weakest. I found that this process led to better development of my ideas before implementation. It also sped up the implementation process, which satisfied my D-personality priorities.

Jerome and I continue to be different in many ways, and we certainly don't always see eye-to-eye. But thanks to DISC, we have a language that helps us honor our unique perspectives and enables us to work together in a much more productive way.

VICKI, FINANCE SERVICE MANAGER

TURNING THEORY INTO PRACTICE

Jack transformed his office using the insights he gained from DISC. He discovered new ways to allow others to express their commitment to work, build positive relationships, and solve problems.

He's never had another problem with his team like he did with Lauren because he's simply more aware of the diversity in how people in his organization approach their work and their relationships. He now has the language and actionable steps to improve how he interacts with others.

We've covered a lot of ground in this book so far. At this point, you have a good idea of the tools we'll be using going forward. Now it's time to turn from theory to practice and learn how these tools can enable you to overcome the specific people problems you and others experience in the work environment.

PART II

MAKING DISC-EQ WORK FOR YOU

Chapter 4

CHECKING YOUR GUT

UNDERSTANDING YOUR DECISION-MAKING

Lisa is one of the brightest up-and-coming managers at the San Diego Humane Society, and it's easy to see why. She has a classic S-style personality. She's warm, friendly, and great at making sure everyone on her team feels appreciated.

When she first entered her current leadership position, though, she walked into a team full of strife. The office was chaotic. Work volume had grown significantly over the past few months, and all the office processes were really stretched. Various people were trying to take control of different decisions, but no one was communicating or collaborating with each other very well.

Lisa's S-related instincts told her that the answer was likely to be found in personal relationships. So she did her best to connect with each person on the team, talk through problems, and listen to every side. Still, the bickering and arguing continued. DISC opened her eyes to why—Lisa's approach was actually adding to the problem instead of resolving it.

She learned that she was allowing her accommodating and empathetic nature to overshadow the team's need for her to make clear and quick decisions. Without clarity and direction from Lisa, the team was drifting, unsure about where to go next.

Making choices that affect others had always been a challenge for Lisa, though she'd never been in a position that accentuated that limitation before. Before stepping into leadership, she strived to preserve the status quo because that was what seemed to make everybody comfortable. She had been the peacemaker, the center of harmony when tense situations arose.

Now, as a leader, she was called upon not just to make peace but to also make choices that would be best for the whole, even when those choices might make some individuals less comfortable. That requirement ran counter to her desire for harmony, and it paralyzed her. And that paralysis affected her overall effectiveness as a leader. She would delay choices or make compromises to soften necessary changes, which slowed down progress and frustrated the very people she was trying to comfort.

Through the DISC framework, she became more self-aware of her behavior and recognized that she had been avoiding decisions because she wanted to avoid hurting feelings.

As her self-awareness increased, Lisa came to realize that the responsibilities of her new role required her to stretch beyond her comfort zone to wisely make the choices her team needed her to make. Although supporting others on her team would always be a priority, Lisa learned she can best demonstrate that support by eliminating the confusion and stress that came from a lack of clear direction.

Increasing her DISC-EQ gave her the language to understand these insights for herself and to share and discuss them with her team. It also provided her with strategies to overcome her tendency to delay choices that would end up being disruptive or uncomfortable for others.

HOW DISC INFLUENCES OUR DECISIONS

In the first part of this book, we looked at DISC-EQ through theory and history, but here, with Lisa, we can see more concretely how DISC-EQ can help real leaders address real challenges associated with the people problem.

Lisa's S-personality gut instinct was to diminish the forcefulness—and the effectiveness—of her decisions in order to avoid disrupting the stable, collaborative atmosphere of her team. This isn't unique to Ss. Decision-making—particularly in time-constrained, high-pressure moments—often minimizes introspection and relies almost exclusively on our "gut." That gut instinct can be one of our best tools in leadership, but when we allow our gut to make our choices without being aware of our own biases, our DISC-oriented limitations can negatively influence the outcome of our decisions. This is true regardless of our position on the DISC wheel.

A D-personality, for instance, often has a natural assertiveness that can make decision-making feel easy. However, if allowed to drift away from strength, that same D-personality can begin to rush decisions without taking the time to involve others or consider relevant data.

An I will share a D's eagerness to make a choice and move on, but that eagerness comes from a different place. Ds want to get results, while Is care about movement, because movement keeps people excited. An I is focused on keeping the team energized and happy. They can end up making decisions like an S—looking for the choice that pleases the most people—but they'll make the decision as quickly as possible.

Like Ss, a C may really struggle to make an initial decision quickly. However, whereas an S is delaying that choice over concerns for how it will affect others, a C worries about getting the decision wrong. It can feel to a C, sometimes, like there is never enough information to ensure that the choice they are making is right. What they might call "not jumping to conclusions" can seem to others like egregious delay.

INSIGHTS: BRETT AND EVANS MAKING DECISIONS

As an S, Evans's difficulty with decisions often mirrors Lisa's. He might delay making decisions or try to soften the blow of those decisions because he instinctively values how others respond more than making the decision quickly. Brett, on the other hand, has to work to avoid allowing his I tendencies to push him into making impulsive decisions too quickly just so he can keep the energy up for himself and others. Choices aren't hard for him to make, but he may make them without thinking through all the consequences.

Increasing his DISC-EQ has given Evans the tools to work through choices more quickly while shifting his focus to what is best for the client, the team, and the organization as a whole. Brett has used his DISC-EQ to remind himself to slow down and ask, "What am I missing? Am I being too impulsive? Am I moving too fast?"

In neither case have we changed who we are or what we value; we've simply learned to manage our gut instincts enough to make sure the choices being made are the best ones we can make.

HOW TO DEAL WITH YOUR GUT

Sometimes our gut instinct leads to effective decision-making. Ds like Vicki in chapter 3 will find that their gut often leads to excellent decisions in moments when quick results are most crucial. Jack in chapters 2 and 3 makes excellent gut instinct choices when he needs to inspire and build momentum. Lisa's instincts will lead her to make choices that improve collaboration, while Cs like our director of operations, Samantha, can trust their instincts to always push for greater accuracy. None of these instincts automatically leads to a better or worse response than the others; they simply align with different priorities and areas of focus.

However, any of these instincts can easily lead to less-than-ideal decision-making in any given circumstance. Vicki (with her D style) can seem impatient and insensitive. Jack (with his I style) can appear to be too impulsive. Lisa (with her S style) can worry too much about how her choices might make people uncomfortable. Samantha (with her C style) can struggle to make a decision at all if there isn't enough data available.

The fact that it's natural to grapple with your personality priorities doesn't mean you have to simply accept the limitations your gut puts on your decision-making. You can learn to counter these impulses when they overrun their usefulness so that you are always making your best decisions.

This starts with raising your self-awareness. Before you can do anything about your gut instinct, you have to know what those instincts are. With DISC, you sharpen your understanding of your personal priorities. Building off that insight, self-awareness can allow you to see whether those priorities are strengthening your decision-making or limiting it.

Examine your recent decisions. Have you made any missteps related to your DISC style? Did you move too quickly? Too slowly? Were you too concerned with the feelings of others? Not concerned enough?

If any of these issues have surfaced for you, you can use DISC-EQ to develop strategies to check those impulses the next time a big decision comes your way. If you are a D, take steps to slow down the process so you can curb that need for closure. Consider whether you are being resolute or insensitive in your choices.

If you are a C, push yourself toward a decision even when you feel there could be more data to review. Search for the balance between weighing all the available information and the need to make a decision so the team can move forward.

Likewise, with Ss and Is, try to balance your emotions with objective criteria to support your natural strengths. An S should try to speed up this process, whereas an I should work to slow it down a bit.

No matter your DISC style, next time you face a tough decision, take a step back, take a breath, and take ten seconds to ask yourself the same basic question: "Are any of my potential limitations coming out in this decision?"

If the answer is yes, or even maybe, it's time to apply these insights to your decision-making process.

Crucially, applying self-awareness and choosing your actions wisely can look different than you might expect. In fact, it can look like doing nothing at all. When applying the lessons of this chapter, you might transition not to action but to inaction in order to stop yourself before you drift from strength to weakness. When you've moved past where your natural tendencies are benefiting the situation, try to rebalance yourself and approach the problem in a new way.

SEEING IT IN ACTION: COMMUNICATING WITH THE BOSS

I'm about as I-personality as it gets. I'm high-spirited, social, and love getting to know my coworkers on a personal level. When I was introduced to DISC, I was not surprised by my style at all. It did, however, open my eyes to how others saw me.

Shortly after I started to build my DISC-EQ, I sat down

at my desk to respond to emails. I had one from my boss, Julie. It read, "Please provide an update on next week's conference." In my I-ness, I wrote her a long, friendly email.

Before I hit "Send," I paused. I thought to myself, "Julie is a very direct, fast-paced, and quick-thinking D."

I looked back at the email she sent to me as well as several others from the past. I noticed most of them were one or two sentences. She definitely had a habit of getting right down to the point. In that moment, I made a decision: I was going to flex some DISC muscles and provide a quick, direct response. I deleted my draft and changed my email. When I finished, it read, simply:

Julie,

We currently have 200 people registered for the conference.

Kelsey

Julie responded within seconds:

Thanks for the quick response. I appreciate it.

My mouth dropped open. She liked it. This was a major eureka moment for me. From that day forward, I always *slow down to consider how other styles may receive my decisions.*

KELSEY, EVENTS PLANNER

ADDING IN THE *OTHER* SIDE

Although improving decision-making largely relies on strong self-awareness, we also need to employ our awareness of others. Part of determining if we need to adjust how we make decisions comes down to whether our decisions are causing problems for others.

Such was the case with Lisa. She realized that her way of making decisions wasn't particularly impacting her, but it was negatively impacting others on the team. Her delays and compromises weren't allowing her to meet the needs of other people. That, ultimately, is why she decided she had to make a change.

As Lisa's story shows, even when we think our decisions are ours and ours alone, in reality they connect to everyone we work with. And, though our DISC style may impact the decisions we make as we think things through, it can have an even bigger impact when we start to communicate with others, as we'll discuss in the next chapter.

D-Personalities

As a D, you likely have a tendency to make decisions in the interest of driving results and pushing things forward. What you might not consider as naturally are the needs of the people impacted by your decisions. As such, before your next big decision, pause for just a moment and make sure you not only think about the results you are trying to deliver but also whom the decision will impact and what they might need related to it. Ask yourself, "What might my S-style colleagues think about if they were making this decision?"

I-Personalities

As an I, you likely have a tendency to get enthusiastic about ideas. When making decisions, you may focus more on the big picture than on the details. Of course, as they say, the devil can be in the details. As such, before your next big decision, pause for just a moment to consider the specifics of what's required to make your decision come to life. Ask yourself, "What might my C-style colleagues think about if they were making this decision?"

S-Personalities

As an S, you likely have a tendency to think about the

people around you when you make decisions. You might also shy away from more risky decisions in the interest of maintaining stability. As such, before your next big decision, pause for just a moment and consider whether you are being bold enough in pushing for results. Ask yourself, "What might my D-style colleagues think about if they were making this decision?"

C-Personalities

As a C, you likely have a tendency to make decisions based on logic and facts. Before making a decision, you likely collect and analyze as much data as you can. The unintended consequence of that research can sometimes be "analysis paralysis," which can lead to decisions taking a long time. As such, before your next big decision, pause for just a moment and see if you can comfortably make a decision based on what you already know (without the need to consider further information). Ask yourself, "What might my I-style colleagues think about if they were making this decision?"

---- *Chapter 5* ----

IT'S NOT JUST WORDS

COMMUNICATING ACROSS STYLES

Over the years, we've had the pleasure of working with some amazing teams and organizations. Recently, we got to know a nonprofit that helps prepare teens for careers in STEM (Science, Technology, Engineering, and Math) occupations. Despite their inspirational mission and their committed team, the organization is not immune to the people problem. Take the small team that coordinates some of their biggest events. Even though all nine individuals are on equal footing as a team, they have not always communicated on equal terms. For one member specifically, her lack of self-awareness led to challenges with the rest of her team.

Brenda was a smart, powerful woman who was passionate about the work she and her team were doing. However, she communicated that passion in a different way than her colleagues. Brenda was an outspoken, fast-paced D on the DISC wheel, whereas her coworkers were all cautious and reflective Cs and Ss.

In meetings, Brenda's focus on action and getting results clashed with the rest of the team's interest in stability and accuracy. The contrast was extreme between the talk-it-through Brenda and the think-it-through members around her.

In meetings, this manifested in very one-sided and unsatisfactory communication for all. Brenda tended to dominate the conversation throughout. She would talk over others and passionately advocate for her ideas. The rest of the team would sit back, largely in silence.

From Brenda's perspective, this was a sign that no one else was pulling their weight. As she saw it, she was the only one introducing ideas and fighting for what she saw as best. From everyone else's perspective, Brenda seemed to be too controlling and bossy, acting as if she were the team leader.

There was resentment on all sides.

This could have turned into another Jack and Lauren situation, but luckily, the team was introduced to DISC-EQ in time. While working through a round of the Appreciation Seat (in which everyone went around the table sharing both an accolade and an idea for how to improve your contribution to the team), Brenda had a eureka moment. She suddenly recognized the root cause of her own people problem. She experienced a transformation right in front of the team.

She stood up and apologized right there. She said, "I'm sorry. For the last couple of years, I've been a jerk. I've been dominating these conversations. I've been getting angry at you and blaming you because you weren't speaking up. I thought I was carrying all the weight, but now I see that I was just taking up all the space for the conversation."

That single step toward flexibility and understanding made all the difference, and the team suddenly found itself on the path toward a healthier and more productive kind of communication.

People problem solved!

"MY COMMUNICATION IS THE RIGHT STYLE"

We tend to assume that the way we see things is the only correct way to see them. With decisions—so long as we are making effective choices—there's little harm in this bias. We are free to feel that our way of making decisions is best, at least for us, so long as the outcomes are sound. We have to leave room for others to make decisions as they prefer, but we aren't usually involved in that internal process.

With communication—and the topics we'll discuss in later chapters—this bias has the potential to poison otherwise healthy relationships. Once damage has been done, it becomes harder to repair those fractured work relationships. It may sound a little silly on the page, but we have all thought at some time, "*I* am communicating in the *right* way; *others* are not." When we approach communication from that position, it becomes a much greater challenge to maintain or reestablish healthy dialogue.

Before we can begin to address miscommunication, we have to recognize that how we communicate is not intrinsically better or worse than how others communicate. Jack and Lauren have already shown us that two people with different styles can mean well, attempt to communicate using their natural styles, and yet still fail to establish and maintain a healthy work relationship because neither is able to honor those differences.

This bias is often at the heart of the people problem. The struggle is not between those who have it right and those who have it wrong. Both parties can have positive intentions. Yet, if neither person can overcome their bias for their own communication preferences and find ways to convey ideas so other people hear it, those good intentions will not save the relationship.

INSIGHTS: COMMUNICATE SO THE OTHER PERSON HEARS YOU

A while back, Evans saw a Facebook post from *Start with Why* author Simon Sinek that read, "Communication is not about speaking what we think. Communication is about ensuring others hear what we mean."[18] This is an idea that we should all think about more often.

People become much more effective at sharing ideas when they move past just saying what they want to say and instead begin to focus on understanding what their audience hears. We have to keep in mind the space between the messenger's intent and the receiver's interpretation when we communicate with anyone, even those we talk to every day. If we only communicate our messages in our style, other people with different styles may easily misinterpret those messages.

YOUR STYLE IMPACTS HOW YOU COMMUNICATE

As we saw in the last chapter, DISC helps us understand how our personal priorities can lead to limitations in our decision-making. This is even truer in communication

18 Simon Sinek, "Communication Is Not about Speaking What We Think," Facebook, October 5, 2014, https://www.facebook.com/simonsinek/posts/communication-is-not-about-speaking-what-we-think-communication-is-about-ensurin/10152771780061499/.

because there's so much more room for misunderstanding between the words we say and how they're heard.

Therefore, before we can look for solutions to manage these limitations, we have to first become more aware of the source of the difficulty. Let's take a look at how the four primary styles are often misread.

C-PERSONALITIES

Ask a C to do some research and present their ideas on how to move a project forward, and you will likely receive a well-thought-out proposal with plenty of facts and data to back up their conclusions.

Yet, because they prefer to consider and analyze information before speaking up, C-personalities can struggle to communicate well with others in the moment. Although Cs can be very effective in giving feedback or presenting their ideas to the team, they are often reticent if not given sufficient time to gather their thoughts and prepare.

This reticence can sometimes look from the outside like disengagement. Those who see participation and contribution as markers of interest in the matter at hand may misread these cues and assume the worst. They might see C-personalities as self-isolating or disapproving when they are simply engaging and communicating *in a different way.*

 ## INSIGHTS: DON'T JUDGE A PARTICIPANT BY HIS REACTION

Years ago, before he knew anything about DISC-EQ, Evans was teaching a multiday workshop. One of the participants, Jonathon, was extremely quiet and appeared disinterested in the course. Other people were very much engaged in the material in more traditional ways—asking questions, responding, and laughing at jokes. He seemed to prefer to sit in the corner and doodle. From Evans's perspective, it seemed that Jonathon was paying no attention at all.

Evans felt frustrated that he wasn't able to reach this person, but luckily, he didn't say anything at the time.

A week after the workshop, Evans received a long, hand-written letter from Jonathon. The letter went on at length about how impactful the class had been for him. In fact, he had already started using the strategies not only at work but also with his wife and kids. In all probability, he may have applied more lessons from the class than anyone else. While Evans didn't recognize it at the time, it turns out that Jonathon was not disinterested. He was just a C-personality who processed the whole class internally.

S-PERSONALITIES

As we saw with Lisa in the last chapter, when S-personalities communicate ideas, they often prioritize how their ideas impact others first. This can be a very positive quality in many situations, but when communication revolves around more analytical ideas—such as the potential financial return on a new project—this reluctance to disagree can lead to frustration on the part of those whose styles are more direct.

Because S-personalities tend to value making everybody comfortable, they may also hesitate to get to their point quickly or directly. They may look for subtler ways to discuss any topic they feel could lead to conflict or inflict some emotional harm.

For instance, when somebody is not fulfilling their potential in their position, S-style personalities can struggle to communicate the necessary feedback. Without awareness of self and others, they might worry more about hurting the person's feelings instead of recognizing the value of providing meaningful direction. Even when they do give constructive criticism, they might communicate it in such a roundabout way that nobody's feelings were hurt, but nobody really knows what the problem is either.

INSIGHTS: WHERE DO YOU WANT TO EAT?

When we are looking for a place to go out to eat, Evans's S-personality really comes out. In fact, it may be the case that Evans has never given a concrete response to the question, "Where do you want to eat?" Instead, he politely goes with, "Wherever you want."

Since Brett's I-personality is also very relationship focused, this can lead to a hunger-inducing delay that goes on for way too long. Both of us care more about our relationship than where we eat, and so, we sit there— famished and unable to communicate a preference.

Usually, Brett's decisive nature breaks the deadlock, and he looks up Yelp reviews to settle the issue for both of us. However, around dinnertime, our duo would probably benefit if one of us channeled a bit more D style and simply said, "We're getting Thai. Let's go."

I-PERSONALITIES

Is, as we know, often thrive on enthusiasm. They get fired up, and they want everyone else to be as excited as they are about whatever topic is being discussed. This can be really useful in communication. It makes people feel better and encourages them to focus on potential upsides, even in the face of dilemmas and downsides.

That excitement, though, can feel suffocating to some. I-personalities don't like leaving empty space in a conversation. It may feel to people with other styles that there's no room to think when an I-style person is around. Like S types, they can also shy away from the tough conversations that involve what they may see as "negative" interaction. If they can find a way to avoid being critical of ideas and of others, they typically will.

At the same time, Is can struggle to maintain focus when that high level of enthusiasm wanes over time. They love new ideas, new conversation topics, and movement. When it comes to ongoing work and the slower and more mundane tasks, they can check out and lose interest.

SEEING IT IN ACTION: I DON'T THINK HE VALUES MY WORK

A few years ago, I was coaching an employee, Jim. He was a high-energy, creative individual with tons of enthusiasm for the projects he was initiating. Then Jim's longtime manager left the organization. Jim was pleased to report to his new manager for whom he had a lot of respect. He would go into their one-on-one meetings and share what he thought were creative and innovative ideas that he believed would help advance the work of their department.

But when Jim would share these new ideas with his manager, the feedback he got tended to be things like, "I'm not sure that will work the way you think it will." Or, "It seems to me you haven't thought this through." Jim would come out of these meetings feeling frustrated and discouraged. He felt like his new manager was overly critical and skeptical of his ideas. Jim began to believe his manager didn't appreciate or value him as an employee.

A few weeks after the new manager started, Jim's entire department took a DISC assessment and debriefed the results with a trained facilitator. What Jim realized was that his enthusiastic I style was very different from his manager's skeptical C style. All of a sudden, what was happening in their one-on-one meetings made a lot more sense. His manager's cautious, detailed approach wasn't intended to be a "buzzkill" to Jim's ideas. Rather, his manager was pointing out things that Jim had not realized and should consider if he wanted his ideas to be all they could be. With that frame of reference, Jim began to view his manager's feedback not as criticism but rather a collaborative effort to help Jim's ideas succeed.

REID, TALENT MANAGEMENT AND
ORGANIZATION DEVELOPMENT CONSULTANT

D-PERSONALITIES

Ds love to cut to the chase so they can get results. If Is are energized by friendly chat, Ds are likely to squash it in the name of efficient communication. Although Ds are irreplaceable for their ability to keep us all on task and moving toward our goals, this sometimes singular focus can leave others feeling a D-personality doesn't care what they think or feel.

All too often, a bit of friendly conversation such as, "How was your weekend?" can be met with a seemingly brusque, "Great, but how's that report coming?"

Very often, Ds don't mean to suggest that they are unfeeling or uncaring toward their colleagues. They simply communicate that caring in a different way. For them, meeting (and even better, *exceeding*) expectations is best for everyone, and they don't want to be embroiled in what they see as the inefficiencies of social niceties.

SEEING IT IN ACTION: SAYING GOOD MORNING

My boss and I both get to work very early, when we are the only two people in the office. For a long time, every morning, I would be at my desk, and he would blow past me. After barely saying good morning, he would close his office door. I was left thinking, "Why does he hate me? What did I do?"

It was very frustrating, and my feelings were hurt every day. Then our department began increasing our DISC-EQ, and I discovered that I am a relationship-oriented S and my boss is a D. The next day, when he blew past my desk again, I was hurt, but then I started thinking about the characteristics of a D. When he is walking to his office, he is probably thinking about all of his tasks for the day. He is in business mode, and his decision not to stop and chat isn't a reflection on me. As soon as I embraced this way of thinking, I no longer took his behavior so personally because I realized it had nothing to do with me.

I still don't understand why he shuts his door, and I chuckle when he does, but it doesn't hurt my feelings. I understand that we are different, and neither one of us is right or wrong, just different in how we approach the day.
MEGAN, PERFORMANCE AND LEARNING CONSULTANT

SEEING THE GAPS IN CONVERSATION

The vast majority of people, regardless of their style, try to use their communication to advocate for what they truly believe is right and best for all.

Whether someone is a D, I, S, or C, miscommunication usually arises not because people are unfocused or unfeeling, but because they are unaware of how their communication style is being perceived. Their goal is to pursue what they believe is the best course of action for themselves and their colleagues, and they try to communicate these beliefs in the method that is most comfortable to them.

For example, the preference of Ds is for action and quick decisions. Ss prefer collaboration and comfort. Ds move fast. Ss prefer a more measured pace. When communicating, these different priorities are naturally going to run into conflict. However, neither style is right or wrong. Both sets of priorities are important and beneficial to a team and an organization. The people problem isn't found just in individual styles; it's in the difficulties inherent in successfully communicating across styles.

So how do we address these differences in communication? What can we do once we are aware of our styles and the styles of others?

We can look for the gaps in conversation, and we can fill

them. This can mean different things to people with different styles. Filling a conversation gap for an I may actually be about leaving space for others to speak. Ds may need to learn to exercise more patience and leave room for conversation even when it feels off topic. For a C or S, it can mean speaking up when they'd rather remain silent.

We have to learn to strengthen our DISC-EQ awareness muscles enough to see the imbalances in conversation and then take appropriate action.

Any personality type can do this. Evans, as an S, does not like to be the one to speak up most in a conversation, but if he's in a room full of Ds and Is—and he has something he really needs to say—he may have to flex parts of his personality that are less natural to him. To make sure he is heard, he may have to work with communication skills, such as assertiveness, that take more focus and effort for him.

This awareness and application needs to take place in all of us. In practice, that means there will be times when we have to step up and be a little more emphatic during our conversation to make our thoughts clear. At other times, we will need to pull back to allow others the space to enter into the discussion and share their ideas.

This can be true with any mixture of DISC personalities.

Sometimes even those who have the same style can actually have a difficult time communicating effectively.

Two Cs, for example, working together on a project may struggle to push a conversation toward decision, since they reinforce their own interest in detailed, meticulous work. Two Ds, on the other hand, may rush to a decision or end up in endless debates trying to prove they are "winning" the argument.

For those conversations to be productive, someone has to be adaptable and flex their weaker communication muscles.

When you have to do something that's out of your comfort zone, it's natural to wish someone else would do it for you. However, you now know that solving the people problem has to start with you. If you don't communicate to others that you are willing to step outside your comfort zone to make sure you are communicating effectively, you can't expect anyone else to fill those gaps in the conversation for you.

SEEING IT IN ACTION: UNDERSTANDING INSTEAD OF ASSUMPTIONS

I'm a solid I, and I work in a nonprofit organization where I collaborate with volunteer groups, stakeholders, and external partners to advance the strategic goals of the organization. In order to foster better relationships between volunteer groups and staff leaders, we recently all took DISC assessments.

I compared my results to one specific external partner, and it was illuminating to see how we were on opposite sides of the "structured" and "unstructured" spectrum. My unstructured tendency is demonstrated through my loose meeting agendas, unscripted approach to dialogue, and ability to pivot with minimal preparation. Contrary to my style, this particular volunteer leader is a highly structured C-personality. He prefers to prep extensively before meetings, asking that agendas be sent a week in advance, and he employs a systematic and predictable process of communication.

Using DISC allowed us to revisit our relationship from a more objective place of understanding, rather than relying on assumptions. Recognizing this difference has significantly enriched my relationship with this stakeholder. I've since found that I've been more inclined to

adapt to meet my partner's style. Having a keen under-
standing of each other's operating styles and tendencies
has allowed us to be more effective leaders together.
KENDALL, SENIOR DIRECTOR OF LEADERSHIP
AND ORGANIZATIONAL DEVELOPMENT

COMMUNICATION HEALS CONFLICT

If you want to improve communication with others, your focus has to be on the changes you can make to improve the situation. It's not about what somebody else needs to change. The surest way to improve your work relationships is by changing your own behavior first.

Clear communication is necessary for productive work, but more than that, when communication becomes miscommunication, the result can lead to unhealthy conflict. For Brenda, that conflict hadn't broken out into direct confrontation, but there was clear resentment on all sides. Once she became more aware of how she was dominating conversations, she flexed her communication muscles and made space for others to contribute more readily. Her actions reduced tension all around and enabled the team to work in a healthier, more collaborative manner.

There's no way around having some conflict in a work environment, since at its core, conflict is rooted in people having different opinions and points of view. Rather than trying to remove all conflict from the workplace, our goal should be to channel those different perspectives in a positive and productive direction. How to do that is what we'll tackle next.

APPLY IT YOURSELF: COMMUNICATING WITH OTHERS

D-Personalities

You may have a tendency to "cut to the chase" when you communicate. Use these strategies when communicating with others:

- With Ds: Stay open to the other person's perspective and points of view
- With Is: Try to make a personal connection
- With Ss: Be aware of their feelings and don't overpower them with your forcefulness
- With Cs: Ask for their insights and let them demonstrate their expertise

I-Personalities

You likely place a lot of value on cultivating relationships when you communicate. Consider using these strategies when communicating with others:

- With Ds: Get to the point quicker than you otherwise might
- With Is: Go ahead and be social but make sure you don't brush off any issues that need to be addressed
- With Ss: Slow your pace and don't overwhelm them
- With Cs: Give them more time to open up as they aren't likely to share personal information as quickly as you

S-Personalities

You may be comfortable staying quiet and letting others take the lead. Consider these strategies when communicating with others:

- With Ds: Be direct with your thoughts and opinions
- With Is: Increase your pace and enjoy making a personal connection
- With Ss: Connect on your shared interest in supporting others
- With Cs: If they come across as questioning or skeptical, remember that they are naturally interested in understanding the logic behind ideas

C-Personalities

You likely aren't as naturally sociable as other people. Consider using these strategies when communicating with others:

- With Ds: Increase your pace and try not to get bogged down in what may be seen as unnecessary details
- With Is: Even if you don't want to share details of your own personal life, go ahead and ask them about theirs
- With Ss: Be mindful that your objective nature may come across as insensitive or impersonal
- With Cs: Go ahead and get into the details and connect on your shared interest in logic

---- *Chapter 6* ----

THE RIGHT KIND OF DISAGREEMENT

CREATING PRODUCTIVE CONFLICT

Success at work requires challenge and change on an ongoing basis. We are constantly considering new products and services, new requirements from our customers, and new improvements in our ability to deliver on the expectations of our stakeholders. We need the best answers and ideas to help us succeed each day, which requires us to challenge our assumptions and vigorously debate new approaches and answers. In this ever-changing environment, our communication differences can make it more difficult to get these issues resolved effectively.

Such was the case at a prominent healthcare organization in California, where a team of twenty individuals were working in a stress-filled, constantly changing environment. Many of the biggest stressors developed out of the same kind of minor differences we've seen elsewhere in this book. In particular, the style of one D, Darren, clashed with the largely reserved styles of the rest of the team.

Darren was brought up to be loud. His family was very loving, but they were noisy and opinionated, and their dinner conversations were often filled with spirited debate. That's just how they expressed themselves. On his own, Darren could be warm, open, and charming because of those qualities, but when part of a team, his vocal and aggressive debating style left many feeling uncomfortable, unheard, and resentful.

In this group, Darren's approach to debate was a little too spirited for some of the others on the team. Darren's assertive style effectively silenced them, leaving meetings dominated by his voice alone. Frequently, when Darren would offer ideas, others would just let their objections go rather than risk getting into an uncomfortable debate. Several members of the team responded not by discussing this imbalance with Darren but by talking among themselves and starting to gang up against him.

Destructive conflict in an office doesn't have to involve shouting matches. Sometimes it shows up as silence. In either case, there's often plenty of gossip as well. That's what happened in Darren's office. The rest of the team was channeling their frustrations into mean-spirited, unproductive conversations that Darren wasn't party to.

Different strategies had been employed to reduce some of this friction, but nothing seemed to defuse the angst felt around the office. The group needed someone to step up and make a significant, positive change to move the group forward.

That person turned out to be Darren himself. For a long time, Darren had been largely unaware of the tension his style was bringing to the team. Like Brenda in the last chapter, he saw himself as passionate and engaged, not overwhelming or combative. He knew he was forceful in sharing his ideas, but unbeknownst to him, his team of quiet, science-and-data-focused Cs and Ss found this behavior disruptive.

Things began to change when HR organized a team event and Darren took an online DISC assessment. The information in his personalized report built up his awareness about his style and how his behaviors might be received by people with different styles. DISC revealed to Darren what the others were uncomfortable telling him: the potential limitations of his personality style were materializing, and they were having a stifling impact on the entire team. When he realized how his colleagues were perceiving his actions, he was embarrassed. And he wanted to make it right.

Darren began with a public apology for his behavior. Then he went further.

He told the team, "I'm not great at seeing when I've crossed the line. So I need your help. If you see me getting too loud and shutting you or others out of the conversation, please interrupt and let me know. With your support, I know I can be a better collaborator with you all."

Darren knew he had to stretch beyond his normal communication style, and he was ready to try. His willingness to be vulnerable and ask for help served to mend a lot of broken relationships. That was an important first step, but alone, it wasn't going to solve the people problem in his office. Getting the team to a new and more productive place would also require Darren's colleagues to stretch, too. Those Ss and Cs who would rather stay silent or walk away from conflict had to learn to speak up and help Darren recognize when he was going too far or was being too abrasive.

It would take some time for everyone to adjust. But with the issue now on the table and out in the open, the team could address it head-on in a productive way. Darren made some mistakes, but the team could tell he was trying. He reacted positively when coworkers brought up issues, and he developed more sensitivity to detect when people were getting uncomfortable.

And those more reserved people on the team? They grew and improved, too. They came to recognize that they could be more valuable to the team by speaking up versus shutting down. Although none of them will ever likely reach Darren's level of assertiveness, they certainly became more comfortable with making their thoughts and opinions heard.

SEEING IT IN ACTION: ONE-TO-ONE INTERACTIONS

Our management team scheduled one-to-one meetings with each other to discuss our DISC profiles. This proved to be very valuable for me and my deputy director, Eunjoo. I'm an S-personality. I value consistency and diplomacy, and I care deeply about the people I work with. I like to process information carefully, and I usually avoid making hasty decisions. Eunjoo, in contrast, is a D-personality. She speaks up about issues and tackles them head-on.

In our one-to-one meeting, Eunjoo and I discussed our respective styles, and we zeroed in on how we interact with each other during times of conflict. Eunjoo observed that she sometimes doesn't know my intentions or my position on an issue. I explained that when confronted with a difficult decision, I feel like I need to consider the range of options available before committing. I also want to be fair and unbiased, so I don't always articulate my views at the outset.

After further discussion, we agreed that Eunjoo would encourage me to share my opinions sooner, even if they might evolve over time as I learn more about how various options would impact the team and organization. I also shared with her that I very much valued her opinions and appreciate when she asked me questions that challenge my thinking, which honored one of her natural tendencies.

The bottom line is that Eunjoo and I provide a good balance for each other, and DISC helped us recognize it.

KEN, AGENCY DIRECTOR

PRODUCTIVE VERSUS UNPRODUCTIVE CONFLICT

Our workplaces have a conflict problem. Just consider these findings from a study on workplace conflict:[19]

- Over a quarter of all employees (27 percent) have been involved in a workplace disagreement that led to personal insults or attacks, while a similar percentage (25 percent) have seen conflict lead to sickness or absence.

---

19   CPP, "Workplace Conflict and How Business Can Harness It to Thrive," *CPP Global Human Capital Report*, 2008.

- Over half of all employees (57 percent) have left a conflict situation with negative feelings, most commonly demotivation, anger, or frustration.
- Over three-fourths of all employees (76 percent) have gone out of their way to avoid a colleague because of a disagreement, creating a distraction for their team.

These findings underscore the human toll of unproductive conflict, which should be reason enough to find a solution. But this is about more than emotional stress; this is also about the bottom line. Negative conflict carries a tangible business cost. Consider these additional data points:

- US employees spend 2.8 hours per week dealing with conflict. This amounts to approximately $359 billion in paid hours (based on average hourly earnings of $17.95), or the equivalent of 385 million working days.
- More than one-third of employees say that negative conflict resulted in someone leaving the company. And turnover is expensive, especially when we consider the full cost of things such as lost productivity and the resources spent to hire and train new employees.

So what is the source of all this unhealthy conflict? Although there are a wide range of factors for sure, one rises to the top. According to that same study, almost half of all employees around the world blame the negative conflict they experience at work on personality clashes (for Americans, that number rises to 62 percent). As we have already seen, our communication preferences and behavioral patterns can lead us to misunderstand each other and even question each other's motives and underlying thoughts. This inability to interact productively with people who have different personality styles stifles business results, undermines team cohesion, and causes not only personal frustration but, in many cases, actual health issues. It is not an understatement to say that unproductive conflict is a cancer in our organizations.

Looking at Darren's story, it's easy to see how having low DISC-EQ can trigger disruptive conflict in the workplace, leading to fractured relationships, unhappy workers, and business inefficiency.

But the act of conflict—the act of disagreeing—doesn't have to be emotionally distressing or organizationally disruptive. Conflict, done right, can be a healthy part of a positive work experience. In fact, if you think about it, conflict is *required* to make sense of competing ideas and diverse perspectives. Conflict is the means by which we discuss options and select the best answers.

If your team doesn't engage in a generous amount of spirited discussion and debate, you may be in real trouble. If you don't have conflict, how are you deciding which actions to take as a team or organization? Is everyone simply agreeing to the first idea that comes up? Of course not. That's why you need to learn how to make conflict productive.

"Conflict" has many different meanings and connotations, some of which are certainly inappropriate for the workplace. For example, we would never suggest that you can solve the people problem by escalating a disagreement to outright warfare.

But another, much less hostile definition calls conflict, simply, a mental struggle over an idea from opposing perspectives. With that description, is there any question that conflict will always be part of our work environments?

In a healthy workplace, workers feel comfortable engaging in productive conflict on a regular basis. Conflict proves you and your colleagues are generating new ideas that people care about. It proves your team is engaged enough to wrestle with those ideas and push for the vision they see as best for the organization. That kind of conflict is productive because it produces the results you want.

On the surface, we can struggle to identify when conflict is productive or unproductive. In both instances, people can speak passionately and disagree deeply. What separates productive conflict from unproductive conflict, then, isn't necessarily how intensely people disagree but how they go about conducting the exchange.

Productive conflict directly addresses the issues where people have differences of opinion or points of view. Unproductive conflict moves from the substance of the issues at hand to attacking others' personalities and behaviors. In productive conflict, the debate can be lively and impassioned, but it remains focused on the issue that needs to be discussed. Those involved seek to find the right answer, not just to win the argument or gain individual glory. At the end, even if disagreement still exists, people can walk away feeling heard and respected.

Unproductive conflict often has less to do with the facts of the debate than with the behaviors and styles of the parties involved. This usually doesn't start with an act of ill will. Far more often, as in the case of Darren and his team, a clash of DISC styles is at the root of the conflict. When differing communication styles are not recognized and accounted for, we increase the odds of people feeling irritated or pushed aside. Instead of respectfully debating the issue, unchecked emotions quickly escalate the interaction into a fight between individuals and their personalities. As the conflict grows deeper, factions can form and sides can be taken. Very quickly, negative conflict can degrade into an everybody-against-one or one-group-against-another dynamic. This becomes a vicious circle making it more difficult to respectfully discuss the real issues that need to be addressed.

SEEING IT IN ACTION: CHANGING HOW I COMMUNICATE AT WORK

My supervisor and I had been struggling to communicate since the day she was hired at our animal care facility. Whenever I had any questions about how we were handling an animal's treatment, my questions would lead to disagreements and arguments. Somehow, things would always get personal and turn negative, and the questions would never get resolved. I came to think that my supervisor didn't like me, and I started to avoid her. At the time, we were a small team. The rest of the team knew that the supervisor and I had issues, and they stopped being comfortable talking with her as well.

The whole team struggled until we took a DISC assessment. Then I learned that my supervisor didn't dislike me; she just communicated differently than I did. I am a very direct and fact-focused D. For some reason, I just expected her to take the same approach. However, I learned that as an S, she was more sensitive. My approach made her feel attacked and defensive. To improve our relationship, I needed to be more aware of how my words might make her feel.

Now, instead of coming into her office looking for immediate facts, I say, "Can you explain this situation to me?"

Or, "Hey, I was wondering if you have any more infor-
mation about Fluffy and his pathway."

Since I began taking her feelings into consideration, our
relationship has improved. And that improvement has
made the entire team closer and more productive.

CASSANDRA, ANIMAL CARE PROFESSIONAL

HOW STYLE AFFECTS CONFLICT

Not every negative conflict comes from a clash within the DISC framework. Some disputes arise out of deeply held beliefs and ideas. Even in these clashes of mental perspectives, however, it is easy to see that low DISC-EQ among those involved impedes the positive sharing of ideas.

When negative conflict *does* arise out of DISC-style tensions, it is often not a matter of vastly different beliefs but of different priorities and mindsets. An I and a C may agree in principle on a potential solution, but their motivations behind that solution can clash. The I may focus on whether that choice will drive action, whereas the C may prioritize the accuracy of the decision over the speed at which things happen. If neither person can recognize the perspective of the other, the solution may be lost as the negative conflict escalates.

Yet, if they both employ a little DISC-EQ and take a step

back, they may find that they are more in sync than it at first appears. The C may realize that the I doesn't want to move ahead with a bad idea; she just doesn't like to spend much time working through all the details. And the I may see that the C wants to move forward, just not until all the i's are dotted and the t's are crossed. When these seemingly competing priorities are made known, the opportunity to work together becomes clear. The final solution, in this case, might be to move a tad slower than the I would like in order to offer a bit more time for the C to reconfirm the accuracy of the plan. By stepping out of their own perspectives, both parties are likely to recognize that the strength of the other serves to create a better ultimate outcome.

Negative conflict rooted in personality styles, however, doesn't occur only between people in different quadrants of the DISC wheel. Sometimes people with similar DISC profiles will run into problems as well. When two Ss disagree, for instance, their preference to avoid confrontation can convert what otherwise might be a simple misunderstanding into a long-term obstacle in their work relationship. A pair of Cs might get bogged down with analysis, trying to prove their respective points. Two Ds may take a minor disagreement and blow it up into a contest over who can win the argument. Two Is could take a different route, injecting a lot of emotion into a reason-based debate and releasing their frustrations through gossip later.

When dealing with any conflict situation, you will be far more successful in navigating it if you are aware of how each person's underlying mindset is influencing their thoughts and actions. By increasing your DISC-EQ, you can better recognize and accept the fact that people with different personality styles look at the same situation through different lenses. The inability to come to terms with this basic human reality is at the heart of why 62 percent of American workers blame negative workplace conflict on personality styles.[20]

Awareness of these mindset differences can equip us to approach conflict situations with more skill and empathy. Rather than digging in on our own perspective, we can step outside of ourselves for a moment and try to understand how the other person is interpreting the situation.

To be clear, we are not saying that the next step is to necessarily give in or even agree with that other perspective. But if you can *see those differences* and acknowledge where the other person is coming from, you gain the ability to *honor those differences* as something that naturally exists between us as human beings. By having this awareness and applying it when needed, you are more likely to defuse any high emotions that may be building, giving you the best chance of preventing conflict from turning destructive.

---

20 Ibid.

INSIGHTS: DOUBLING DOWN ON DISC

Our response to conflict can be influenced by many factors, including everything from family upbringing to cultural heritage and personal experience. However, doubling down on our DISC style is the path most of us take when things get heated. Given the power of our emotions to override rational thought (as we covered in chapter 2), this makes sense.

The tendency of a D-personality to bring problems up with an eye on getting answers quickly often leads, in moments of frustration, to turning aggressive and trying to overpower others in the conversation. S-personalities tend to favor harmony, so they are likely to attempt to alleviate conflict by pulling back and biting their tongue, leaving their own feelings unaddressed.

Because Cs value objectivity, they can become coldly logical and impersonal in moments of conflict. Or they can retire from the conversation entirely. Is, on the other hand, might want to move on from a conflict as quickly as possible instead of addressing the underlying issue simply because it feels uncomfortable and saps their natural energy.

UNMET NEEDS CAN TRIGGER UNPRODUCTIVE CONFLICT

When we engage in discussions in which people have different points of view, we can get caught up in making sure our own needs get met. When this happens, we can easily neglect the emotional and psychological needs of others in the discussion. A D may assert that a decision has to be made, and it is time to put aside incoming information. That could potentially alienate a C who struggles with quick decisions and uses data analysis as a way to get comfortable with moving a project forward. Situations like these can lead to frustration on the part of those who feel their emotional needs are not being honored.

As frustration rises, that sense of being unaccommodated can push a conflict that was initially focused on the issues at hand into an area that is unproductive and personal. That was the case with Chris, an IT professional, and his new team leader, Linda. Chris was an insightful, diligent C-personality whose contributions had historically been valued by his organization. He'd work late into the night and over weekends to make sure he always gave his customers the right answer. He was comfortable putting in the time to ensure the system provided accurate and stable information to meet the needs of the organization.

However, when Chris began working with Linda, conflict quickly began to develop. It started productively enough, with Chris bringing up various technical issues that he thought were a problem in how the system was functioning. But when Linda brushed aside his concerns, Chris took it personally, and the conflict turned negative. From his perspective, his knowledge and experience were unappreciated, and that hurt.

In reality, Linda did appreciate Chris's expertise, but her low DISC-EQ interfered with her ability to express it effectively. She was an I-personality who tended to avoid uncomfortable, stressful discussions and preferred to focus on big picture over details. Falling prey to her DISC-style limitations, she glossed over Chris's concerns in an effort to keep the project moving forward and the work environment positive.

Since they weren't self-aware enough to recognize the underlying difference in perspective, Chris and Linda continued to struggle. The conflict lingered and tension rose. Chris became aggressive and passionate over any disagreement, even shouting and refusing to move on until others submitted to his arguments. Linda became increasingly frustrated with Chris, all the while not realizing that her own actions were influencing his increasingly combative attitude.

As part of working with Chris and Linda, we made them aware of their own DISC styles, including the common limitations associated with being an I and a C, which helped them understand what was contributing to the growing hostility between them. Once Linda recognized that she had been overlooking Chris's needs, she was able to adjust her approach. At the same time, Chris became more aware of his stressors and learned to find more productive ways to respond when they were triggered.

 **INSIGHTS: REGRETS VERSUS REPERCUSSIONS**

Language is incredibly important when building DISC-EQ, and when we do not appreciate its nuance, we can struggle to absorb its advice.

During one of Evans's executive coaching engagements, he was working with a strong D-personality. As they discussed her behaviors during conflict, she stopped him and said, "That's not right. You are wrong about what happens."

"What do you mean?" Evans asked.

"You implied that I say things that I regret," she said. "That never happens."

Rewording the concept, Evans asked, "Do you ever say things that cause repercussions you don't like?"

"Oh yes," she said, "that happens every day."

That was a self-awareness eureka moment for her, as she suddenly recognized her tendency to focus on her own needs without taking time to consider the perspective of others. Since that day, she's challenged herself to increase her DISC-EQ and to strive to adapt her behaviors for the mutual benefit of everyone on her team.

HOW WE MAKE CONFLICT HEALTHY

A workplace dominated by artificial harmony—where issues are pushed aside or glossed over in an attempt to keep the peace—is almost as bad as one filled with unproductive conflict. You *want* people to engage in energetic, ideas-focused conflict in your workplace every day. You *want* to see productive and respectful debates in which everyone feels included and everyone contributes to the ultimate choices made around the office.

In order to transition unhealthy conflict into its productive counterpart, we need to address the root misunderstandings between ourselves and other parties. Because every conflict has at least two sides, we have to begin our introspective process by expanding our self-awareness and considering how *we* might be making the situation more challenging. Stepping back to review our own actions can give us the space to act more deliberately and choose our next response more wisely. Instead of exacerbating a negative conflict, we can de-escalate or, if need be, walk away to let tensions cool.

When you take responsibility for your actions rather than assigning blame to others, you provide yourself the emotional space to see different perspectives and to adapt your style to make sure your perspective is heard in the way you intend it to be.

You can do this by applying the following two-step process to yourself and encouraging your teammates to do the same.

Before we begin, an important note: you should work through this process *before* you are in the swirl of a heated discussion, as it is tough to think and reflect when you are in the middle of the storm. This process is a preventative measure, not necessarily a solution for a team already in the midst of negative conflict.

Step one is to become aware of your own reactions and behaviors during conflict situations. Reflect on some difficult conversations that you have been involved in recently. Your first thought might be that another person in the situation was the problem, but you need to remember you can only make change happen by starting with yourself. You may feel someone else's words or deeds caused the conflict, but you can't control what another person chooses to say or how they choose to act. You can only control how you respond to it.

Think about how you might have handled things differently if you applied some extra awareness of yourself and the others involved in the conflict. Make a list of things you said or did that may have contributed to the unproductive nature of the situation. You can use the DISC insights we've shared for reference, but remember that conflict can bring out a wide range of behaviors in all of us. Really challenge yourself to understand how you might have played a part in things not going well. You don't have to show the list to anyone else, so go ahead, be completely honest.

Then, in step two, armed with the benefit of self-reflection, decide how you want to respond in the future. What choices will you make to act in a way that keeps the conflict healthy and productive, improving the communication and decisions for the group? Commit to those changes and remember your commitment the next time you start to sense that conflict is shifting from productive to unhealthy.

This isn't a one-time exercise, and you shouldn't expect to expertly avoid every unproductive reaction in your next moment of frustration or tension. Instead, think of this process as a feedback loop for yourself as you work on improving your skills in conflict situations. Repeat steps one and two after every situation that did not go as well as you would have liked. Take the time to reflect and see how you can more productively help the conversation the next time. You can keep a journal and record how each conflict evolves and how effectively you improved your own responses. A journal can help you maintain motivation and keep the process at the top of your mind.

When you are ready, you can take this one step further by sharing your goals with your colleagues and asking them to help hold you accountable, just as Darren did in the opening story of this chapter. Gather together a few people in your work environment whom you trust to be honest with you. Then ask them, "Are there things that I do that make it more difficult for us to reach a resolution? What do I do that gets in the way of our communication and our work together?"

Since every person has a somewhat limited or biased view of themselves, it's very likely that these people will see qualities you display that you aren't aware of. The truth for most of us is that we aren't always aware of our own tendencies, particularly in moments of conflict, when our minds are focused elsewhere.

Expressing your desire to improve your behaviors during conflict can lead to several benefits. You commit to self-improvement, and others commit to helping you achieve that goal. In turn, they are more likely to open themselves up to the same process of self-improvement.

INSIGHTS: THE REWARD AND RISK OF THE THIRD-PARTY INTERMEDIARY

When you are in the throes of an ongoing conflict, it can be useful to practice your responses with an impartial third party. An outside party can help those in conflict to prepare and practice for a potentially uncomfortable conversation in which disagreements are addressed and resolved. Under these circumstances, the third party can defuse some of the heightened emotion and resentment lingering from the previous conversation so that all parties can more effectively reach a positive resolution.

Unfortunately, people in the middle of unproductive conflicts frequently bring in a third party for other purposes. For example, they might attempt to bring in an outsider as an ally who sees things from their perspective. In such cases, the outsider is rarely an unbiased third party. They might gossip and complain instead of looking for productive strategies to overcome differences in opinion.

In that situation, the third party is really only making matters worse because they are reducing the likelihood the people in conflict will speak openly, and they are further entrenching the frustrations on all sides.

BUILDING HEALTHY CONFLICT IS A TEAM SPORT

Certain kinds of conflict are good and improve the team. It is crucial that organizations work through tough choices, and healthy conflict enables that to happen. Allowing a discussion to get mean spirited or disrespectful, however, is not productive and will often lead to bigger issues. We must remember that work is always a team sport. When conflict arises, everyone on the team is affected. Negative, emotionally charged interactions—even when between just two people—typically spirals out to others in the workplace, reducing team engagement and hindering progress on important objectives.

So the best approach for controlling unproductive conflict is naturally a team-based solution. To solve the people problems in today's work environment, then, we have to discover how to apply DISC-EQ to find the best, most productive ways to communicate and interact. When we make the team our priority, we all rise together. We communicate better, engage in productive debates, and ultimately, achieve more impactful results.

APPLY IT YOURSELF: CONFLICT

All people, though some more than others, engage in unproductive behaviors during conflict. You must know what your unproductive tendencies are, and you must control them. Further, you must stay consciously aware that style differences themselves can add tension to any conflict situation and can sometimes overwhelm and exacerbate the underlying issue. Use the tips below to recognize your own tendencies and to develop more productive behaviors with others.

D-Personalities

You may have a tendency to be blunt and outspoken during conflict. Use these strategies when engaging in conflict with others:

- With Ds: Focus on resolving the issue rather than winning
- With Is: Hear them out and let them know that the underlying relationship is still strong
- With Ss: Don't interpret their silence as agreement, as they might not be quick to share their thoughts
- With Cs: Support your arguments with data and give them time to present their side

I-Personalities

You may tend to avoid confrontation for fear of damaging the relationship. Consider using these strategies when engaging in conflict with others:

- With Ds: Make your case objectively rather than letting emotions take over
- With Is: Let them know that disagreement now doesn't mean a poor relationship going forward
- With Ss: Don't gloss over disagreements; address the issues directly
- With Cs: State your case factually, and don't insist on an immediate resolution

S-Personalities

Arguing your point might not come easy to you, and you may tend to be overly accommodating. Consider these strategies when engaging in conflict with others:

- With Ds: Avoid giving in to their demands just to regain harmony
- With Is: Let them know that facing the disagreement now will help maintain a good relationship down the road
- With Ss: Be aware that holding in your feelings could be more harmful than speaking candidly
- With Cs: Be assertive about your own needs, and don't just give in to their logical arguments

C-Personalities

You may be frank and unemotional when making your point. Consider these strategies when engaging in conflict with others:

- With Ds: Focus on resolving the issue rather than winning
- With Is: Suggest logical ways to resolve the issue, and don't withdraw if things get emotional
- With Ss: Remember that you may have to ask a few times before they'll tell you what's really bothering them
- With Cs: Focus on resolving the issue respectfully rather than on proving you are right

---

Chapter 7

MAKING THE TEAM WORK

DISC IN THE TEAM SPACE

The Business Resource Center (BRC) made reducing negative conflict one of their primary organizational goals. BRC is the agency that provides technical support across the government for King County, Washington. They support several major IT systems that are used by multiple agencies to provide services to people throughout the region. With a mission that affects thousands of members of their vast community, the leaders at BRC strive to create conditions ideal for teams across the organization to work effectively together.

Their ambitious plan grew out of an agency-wide DISC assessment, which showed that a wide variety of DISC styles were represented across the BRC workforce but that these styles weren't always communicating effectively to one another. This raised many concerns, but there was one stark difference the leaders at BRC knew they needed to address. The majority of the workforce were more methodical and reserved C and S styles. However, these people often struggled in smaller group meetings in which their more dynamic and fast-paced I and D colleagues tended to dominate discussions.

Guided by the common language of DISC, BRC deployed a set of conflict-reducing strategies across the whole organization. They started by posting a six-foot DISC wheel on the wall outside the director's office with every employee's name plotted in the proper quadrant. They also made the DISC assessment results public and encouraged coworkers to sit down with each other and discuss the details and insights. This action served to put the concept of personality styles out in the open, which in turn cultivated greater self-awareness and offered an easy way to learn about each other's tendencies and preferences.

In addition to supporting awareness, the leadership committee put structures in place to support all styles on the team. For instance, managers, supervisors, and project leads were instructed to start sharing agendas and materials the day before a meeting so that those who preferred to have more time to process information were not at a disadvantage.

To further improve interoffice communication and empower

everyone to participate in conversations, they also adopted the "Step Up and Step Back" approach. This strategy drew upon the DISC-EQ model, pushing team members to become more *aware* of DISC-style attributes and encouraging them to *apply* that knowledge to make wiser choices and to adapt their behavior for mutual benefit. Those who were more reticent to engage in some circumstances were urged to "step up," whereas those who were typically most eager to speak up in debates were asked to "step back" and leave room for others to make their thoughts known. During meetings, participants were encouraged to comment whenever they noticed a small number of team members dominating a discussion. That way, someone could ask those prominent speakers to *step back* and leave room for others. Likewise, everyone was asked to point out when parts of the group had gone silent and to invite those quieter members to *step up* into the conversation.

In combining these strategies, BRC has been able to improve communication and increase productivity across the organization, while also raising team member engagement.

TEAMS ADD MORE VARIABILITY, VOLATILITY, AND OPPORTUNITY

Introducing multiple people with varied and unique personalities and experience will always increase the potential for both success and struggle. We've seen how complex decisions are when we make them alone and how challenging communication and conflict can be between just two individuals. In teams, we are dealing with multiple people with different styles, as well as all the interactions those various styles create.

In many of our previous examples, we focused on how one individual made a change. However, under most circumstances, in a team environment, the whole team needs to commit to evolving together. That's why, in this chapter, we will talk about how you can make change happen for a group of people. Given a large enough team, every style and priority may be present and, often, multiple times. And the larger and more diverse the team, the more opportunities you have for poor decision-making, miscommunication, and unproductive, emotionally disruptive conflict.

This may sound bleak, but luckily, the upside of teamwork is far greater than the downside. Teamwork has become the most irreplaceable system of organization in most businesses for a reason: it brings about the best results. When a team is running well, it can harness the strength of every member. That's why, casting our eye to the years ahead, we can expect that teams are likely to become more everpresent in every workplace.

Artificial intelligence, automation, and other technological advances have reduced the space for more individualized work. What a computer can do without human involvement, a business simply won't ask a person to do anymore. The one kind of work a computer or machine can't replicate—and may never be able to replicate—is interactive teamwork. Our role in the workplace now revolves around that interpersonal interaction where the best ideas come together.

This is not welcome information to everyone. Many workers would rather return to a time when they could work quietly and alone, keeping their heads down. But even in positions that once had fewer social requirements, the space for truly independent work is shrinking.

Consider information technology (IT) workers. We all know the stereotype about IT professionals, the ones who would lock their office doors to keep others out if they could. If that stereotype was ever accurate, it isn't anymore. Increasingly, these tech experts are required to collaborate with colleagues on interconnected development projects. They have to be able to explain how to utilize hardware, software, and applications to others in the business. They probably need to interact with clients—internal or external—on a regular basis.

IT is just one example of this phenomenon. As team-based collaboration continues to become central to jobs in every industry, our ability to work as a team will become ever more important. In other words, effective team building and team maintenance affects all of us and will continue to do so no matter our position.

SEEING IT IN ACTION: CONNECTING THE TEAM THROUGH CHALLENGE

I'm a solid C in charge of a team of marketing managers who are also all Cs. Not too long ago, our company went through a reorganization, and my C-dominated team now reports to a new director who is a hard-core D.

So how do we make this work? Well, it primarily revolves around a trait Ds and Cs share: challenge. It's taken a bit to communicate this up to my director and down to my reports, but we've arrived at this sometimes-tense-but-always-friendly place where my director provides prioritization for everything so that her most pressing requests are addressed first, and my team and I can challenge accelerated timelines and requests that are sometimes vague.

My director acknowledges that my C teammates want to go slow to avoid mistakes, while also lovingly pressing us to get her top priorities done quickly. At the same time, my reports realize that with marketing goals and tools that are constantly changing, when the work is "good enough" by our standards, it's usually excellent as far as our director is concerned.

There was some misunderstanding initially, but thanks to our collective emotional maturity and knowledge of DISC, we all reached this common ground together.

JASON, MARKETING MANAGER

SIGNS A TEAM ISN'T WORKING

Team dysfunction isn't always easy to spot, particularly since it doesn't always show up clearly on a report or in a team's results. A team may achieve reasonable success while still failing to live up to its full potential.

So what does a dysfunctional team look like then?

Thankfully, Patrick Lencioni has outlined this for us in his *New York Times* best seller, *The Five Dysfunctions of a Team.* This leadership fable highlights five factors that are common signs of breakdown in a team: a lack of trust, unhealthy conflict, a lack of commitment, failure to hold each other accountable, and a lack of focus on collective results.

Want to know how well your team is doing? Ask yourself the following questions about these five dysfunctions:

- Do your teammates build trust by recognizing and honoring each other's personality styles?

- During times of conflict, are people on the team respectful of each other's priorities and emotional needs?
- When committing to decisions, does the team ensure that expectations and assignments are communicated clearly enough that all members can fully understand what is required of them regardless of their DISC style?
- Have team members built strong enough relationships to be able to hold each other accountable in a respectful way without needing to involve the boss in the discussion?
- Do all team members feel their opinions and emotional needs are honored such that they can stay focused on the team's goals rather than pursuing other objectives?

If you answered no to any of these, your team likely has some dysfunction. But don't despair. We have good news for you.

IMPROVING THE TEAM

Perhaps unsurprisingly, when we work to directly target and overcome these five dysfunctions, we end up creating the opposite of dysfunction—we create *cohesion*. That is why we spend so much time coaching leaders to take their knowledge of DISC and apply it to these Five Behaviors of a *Cohesive* Team™.[21]

---

21   "The Five Behaviors of a Cohesive Team" is a registered trademark of John Wiley & Sons Publishing.

- Build Vulnerability-Based Trust: In Lencioni's model, trust is the first behavior to ground every successful team. For a team to reach the full potential of all its creative, individual parts, there has to be enough trust for each individual member to feel comfortable sharing ideas, asking for help, and making mistakes. Building up DISC-EQ can help establish that trust. For many teams, a key factor that leads to a lack of trust is not understanding and appreciating the differences team members bring to the table. However, once teammates understand and apply DISC, they are better able to address many of the issues that otherwise might lead to a breakdown in trust.
- Engage in Productive Conflict: By honoring differences and developing deeper trust, teams are better able to step into conversations that embrace healthy conflict around ideas. Teammates can be much more spirited in those conversations, since the exchanges don't turn personal. DISC-EQ helps everyone on the team give each other the space to contribute fully to important decisions for the group.
- Commit to Team Decisions: Teams with high DISC-EQ make and keep commitments by nurturing an understanding of the needs and priorities of the people involved. By improving communication across the board, details about roles, responsibilities, and measures of success can be defined and conveyed much more clearly to everyone on the team, regardless of their DISC style.

- Hold Each Other Accountable: Accountability is a challenge for many teams, and a lack of DISC-EQ is part of the reason. Even after a team gets fully committed to a decision, holding a teammate accountable can be a situation fraught with tension without a solid understanding of everyone's communication preferences and emotional needs. How should I share my feedback? How will it be received? What can I do to ensure it comes across in the spirit intended? By understanding each other through DISC, teams are better equipped to provide helpful feedback to one another.

- Focus on Collective Results: When collective results are top of mind, teammates are quick to recognize the contributions and accomplishments of others. DISC provides guidance on how different team members might like to be recognized, be it a public acknowledgment with lots of fanfare or a private thank-you in a quiet office.

In conjunction with their organization-wide DISC assessment, BRC worked through these Five Behaviors of a Cohesive Team, one at a time. It was hard work over several months, but the results were well worth it.

Any team can replicate BRC's results if they are willing to commit and stay dedicated to the work required. With focus and diligence, even highly dysfunctional teams can find their way back to a healthy, cohesive work environment.

GETTING TO KNOW YOUR TEAM

To find that balance, you have to get to know the members of your team. Before you can make any significant adjustments to your team environment, you have to know what everyone's needs are and whose needs are not being met. DISC is a useful language here.

While assessing and discussing DISC styles, keep an eye on how diverse your team is as well. The majority of your team may consist of one or two styles—very possibly your own. Variety in thought is valuable for every team. If you don't see that within your team environment, that should be something you work to adjust over time.

In the meantime, though, it will be your job to flex your DISC-EQ muscles to ensure the whole team can be successful.

PROJECT TEAMS COUNT, TOO

The above advice—and indeed all the advice in this chapter—applies not just to established teams but to project teams as well. A great deal of work in organizations is done in project teams that exist for only the length of the project. While these teams face challenges unique to their limited scope and duration, it is still enormously valuable to build up the team's DISC-EQ to create healthy, productive working relationships.

One additional challenge often presented by project teams is the lack of a previous history of working together. In that event, it may take a little more time to identify people's style characteristics. However, in truth, this is sometimes an advantage. At times, having a history can make the cooperation more difficult due to baggage in a relationship. In either case, the sooner you introduce DISC-EQ to your team, the quicker you can help your project team move toward maximum cohesiveness and results.

SEEING IT IN ACTION: ENDING THE TENNIS MATCHES

I was fortunate to support a management team of super-smart high achievers. It was surprising to me, then, when our newly formed team of six struggled with managing our own meetings. An observer looking into the room might think four of us were watching a tennis match between the other two. Everyone would leave the room frustrated with the lack of communication, resolution, or progress. The four quieter team members were all C-personalities, whereas the two more vocal members were Ds. My role as a support person had no defined power, and often that meant I was the go-between. I went home exhausted every day!

Our fearless leader introduced us to DISC. We made a

concerted effort to learn our own styles and those of the whole management team. And we began to recognize the source of our breakdown. We made purposeful attempts to build trust and engage in healthy conflict. And it worked.

Since then, the tennis matches have stopped. I am rarely the mediator, and I go home with energy left over!

Our team is about to expand and almost double in size. I'm delighted at the thought of catching the newbies up on DISC and showing them how far we have come!

NANCY, ADMINISTRATIVE ASSISTANT

CREATING GROUND RULES

In her book *Dare to Lead*, Brené Brown writes, "Daring leaders fight for the inclusion of all people, opinions and perspectives because that makes us all better and stronger." We couldn't agree more. You should work with your team to set ground rules that enable and encourage everyone to participate fully in the conversation. Clearly defined team norms will make it known to all what is fair and acceptable—as well as unacceptable—for your meetings and other team interactions, thus creating a space where everyone can feel comfortable expressing themselves.

You can be imaginative here. Should there be a time limit

for how long someone can hold the floor? Do you want your talkative Is and Ds on one side of the table with quieter Ss and Cs on the other so you can better balance speaking time? Should you always review the last meeting's ideas at the beginning of the next meeting, giving your "think it through" teammates an opportunity to share any new thoughts they have? Should you, like BRC, encourage people to Speak Up or Step Back?

In a lecture at Stevens Institute of Technology, Susan Cain—self-professed introvert and author of *Quiet: The Power of Introverts in a World That Can't Stop Talking*—highlighted how extreme the disparity between DISC styles can be in a team environment. Looking at the characteristic of extroversion and introversion, which roughly aligns with the north-south DISC axis of outgoing versus reserved, Ms. Cain stated that today's workplace has a "bias toward extroverts" and allows "the most vocal and assertive people to dominate meetings." Backing up her argument, she cited a Kellogg School of Management study that concluded, "The workplace imbalance between extroverts and introverts is particularly acute in meetings, where three people often do 70 percent of the talking."

If this is the reality on your team and if you are hearing the opinions of only a small percentage of your teammates, how, then, can you expect to make good team decisions? The answer, of course, is you can't, at least not until you find a way to balance out the conversation among everyone, regardless of style. This requires you to get to know your team, create ground rules, establish nurturing language, and of course, embrace your role as a leader and lead the way.

Susan Cain has some excellent advice here. She suggests you encourage people to take some time before a meeting to think about what they want to contribute and to then share those thoughts during the first few minutes after the team is together in person. This allows those ideas to anchor the discussion, which can open the door to having more people feel like important contributors. That little push at the beginning helps reduce how intimidating it can be to speak up. By giving your S and C team members, in particular, the space to speak at a crucial point in the discussion, you may maximize their engagement and the power of their ideas.

INSIGHTS: LESSONS FROM AN EARLY TEAM

After leaving the air force, Evans joined a financial services firm as a department leader. He recalls that those early meetings were dominated by him and two other members. The three of them could fill several flip charts with their ideas while everyone else sat in silence. The rest of the team, Evans found out later, were the source of fantastic ideas, but those ideas were typically voiced several hours after the meeting.

It was only when Evans took the time to get to know his team and create specific ground rules around communication and brainstorming techniques that those ideas could enter into conversation without being overshadowed by the more vocal members of the team.

And good thing, too. As it turned out, from then on, many of the team's best ideas came from the members who initially struggled to get a word in edgewise.

NURTURING LANGUAGE

Ground rules that encourage everyone to share space in the team are a powerful way to begin balancing your team's personalities. To make sure those rules stick, you have to establish an atmosphere of openness and vulnerability through the use of nurturing language.

You can start with how you introduce the need for change. Talk about the benefits of "having a discussion about our styles" instead of announcing a detailed solution from on high. Make it clear that other perspectives are always welcome. Creating a more inclusive, positive environment can begin with something as simple as establishing rules of basic politeness. Remember to say, "Please speak up, as we'd really like to hear your opinion on this," when someone seems hesitant to talk, or "Thank you for that contribution," when a team member makes a recommendation.

You may also be able to reduce unhealthy conflict by stating simply, "You see this in a different way than I do. Let's keep discussing our individual perspectives to see what we can learn from that together."

When you adapt your behavior for mutual benefit, you demonstrate your openness to ideas, your eagerness to hear from everyone, and your assurance that no one's ideas will be considered unworthy of discussion, all of which can lead to a significant increase in participation.

 **SEEING IT IN ACTION: DEVELOPING A WORKING RELATIONSHIP WITH A NEW COWORKER**

When we hired a new strategic planner, I was out on maternity leave and unable to participate in the interview process. The new hire would be my closest counterpart, so I worried whether our personality styles would mesh.

Luckily, when Kris and I met, we immediately found common ground in the struggle of raising young children while working full time. Still, it was clear we had very different communication styles. Kris tended to speak her mind and communicate directly, whereas I often held back and spoke more tentatively.

A few months into working together, Kris and I attended a two-day workshop designed to build up our DISC-EQ. There, we learned that I am an S style and Kris is a D style. We confirmed that our styles naturally communicate differently and that we counterbalance each other well. I'm open to just about any idea that comes across my desk, and Kris is willing to ask tough questions that help separate the best ideas from the rest.

In a way, DISC supported what we already knew about working together. But for me, it has really helped raise my awareness of how to work with people of all different styles and how to view differences as complementary strengths.

HANNAH, OPERATIONS PLANNER

TEAMS NEED DIVERSITY

The best teams are those with a variety of perspectives and experiences. No team benefits from the tunnel vision of a single, unified perspective on how things should be done.

This need to cultivate different views can naturally lead to tension, but when we manage a team effectively, we create a 360-degree view of every challenge. It's healthy for a team to include those looking to move forward and achieve goals quickly, those who want to check everything for accuracy, those who want to improve relationships, and those who want to nurture enthusiasm. Each person brings valuable input to the team process, and their contribution is missed when they feel unable to engage fully.

BRC has become a far more effective organization by encouraging a healthy respect for and expression of different styles. They realized that little could be achieved if one type of communication shut out all the others.

Good teams take work, but DISC arms you with a language and tools to begin the work to make your team great. But what about your work outside the team environment? How do you deploy your DISC-EQ to create positive relationships when speaking with clients and colleagues you rarely see or whom you may never have seen before?

APPLY IT YOURSELF: TEAMWORK

Without at least a moderate level of DISC-EQ, it is common for teammates to view each other through the clouded lens of their own natural DISC style. In such cases, what they see isn't necessarily an accurate account of another person, but rather a biased perspective that "judges" others based on one's own priorities and preferences. The bullets below will help you be more aware of some of the common biases that show up on teams, giving you the power to avoid them.

D-Personalities

How might you see others on your team if your view is overly influenced by your own DISC style?

- You may see Ds as: Driven and assertive
- You may see Is as: Talkative and overly optimistic
- You may see Ss as: Soft-spoken and indecisive
- You may see Cs as: Analytical and private

How might others on your team see you if their view is overly influenced by their own DISC style?

- Ds may see you as: Driven and assertive
- Is may see you as: Outspoken and blunt
- Ss may see you as: Critical and dominant

- Cs may see you as: Intense and demanding

I-Personalities
How might you see others on your team if your view is overly influenced by your own DISC style?

- You may see Ds as: Outspoken and blunt
- You may see Is as: Passionate and adventurous
- You may see Ss as: Careful and patient
- You may see Cs as: Skeptical and unemotional

How might others on your team see you if their view is overly influenced by their own DISC style?

- Ds may see you as: Talkative and overly optimistic
- Is may see you as: Passionate and adventurous
- Ss may see you as: High-spirited and scattered
- Cs may see you as: Emotional and impulsive

S-Personalities
How might you see others on your team if your view is overly influenced by your own DISC style?

- You may see Ds as: Demanding and dominant
- You may see Is as: High-spirited and scattered
- You may see Ss as: Considerate and caring
- You may see Cs as: Precise and reliable

How might others on your team see you if their view is overly influenced by their own DISC style?

- Ds may see you as: Soft-spoken and indecisive
- Is may see you as: Careful and patient
- Ss may see you as: Considerate and caring
- Cs may see you as: Flexible and diplomatic

C-Personalities
How might you see others on your team if your view is overly influenced by your own DISC style?

- You may see Ds as: Intense and demanding
- You may see Is as: Emotional and impulsive
- You may see Ss as: Flexible and diplomatic
- You may see Cs as: Logical and systematic

How might others on your team see you if their view is overly influenced by their own DISC style?

- Ds may see you as: Analytical and private
- Is may see you as: Skeptical and unemotional
- Ss may see you as: Precise and reliable
- Cs may see you as: Logical and systematic

Chapter 8

WORKING WITH THOSE OUTSIDE YOUR CIRCLE

APPLYING DISC-EQ TO CUSTOMERS AND PARTNERS

As an I, Brett has always been great at striking up new relationships. His priorities for action, enthusiasm, and strong connections with others make him a natural-born salesman. He loves nothing more than getting people excited about what we're doing at Integris. In fact, listening to Brett on the phone with another I style can be quite amusing. They'll often chat and laugh about a wide range of topics—many of them personal—before getting down to business.

But Brett has learned that his natural I communication tendencies won't be received as favorably by everyone, so he uses his DISC-EQ to read people and adapt his behavior for everyone's mutual benefit. For example, he will still be chatty with S-personalities, though his pace definitely slows. With Cs, he remains friendly but puts far more focus on supporting the conversation with facts and data. And you can tell when he's speaking with a D because he cuts to the chase much more quickly, getting to the point of how Integris can help drive results.

While a casual observer might think that the adjustments Brett makes just come naturally, the truth is that it's all the result of his efforts to build awareness and apply the concepts of DISC to each interaction.

Making good first impressions and building healthy relationships is central to business success. When we misread people and consequently communicate in an ineffective way, we may come to regret missed opportunities, unhappy customers, or frayed relations with those we are trying to serve. Creating that rapport can be one of the toughest aspects of any job, regardless of whether you are working with people who are external or internal to your organization. However, building up your DISC-EQ will provide the insights and techniques you need to communicate more effectively and build healthier relationships with all those who are outside of your inner circle.

BE MORE THAN A CHAMELEON

Cultivating positive relationships with clients has always been central to sales training. Brett has been involved in sales, customer service, and business development for over twenty years. His career began in the mid-'90s, when he worked in financial services in San Diego. Back then, the big idea was to "be a chameleon." According to this theory, the best salesperson was one who could mirror their customer's personality and behaviors.

People inherently like and trust those whom they feel are similar to themselves, so this theory recommended salespeople simulate that likeness by matching behaviors. If a customer talks fast, a salesperson should speed up the pace of their own speaking. If the customer talks in a slower, more measured voice, the salesperson should match that pace. A salesperson should lean in when the customer leans in, cross legs when the customer crosses legs, and so on.

The problem with using the chameleon as a metaphor is that it can be misinterpreted. Copying and blending in like a chameleon can easily slide into mimicry and mockery. The metaphor also suggests something artificial and misleading when developing a relationship. Our goal should be to inspire our clients and business partners with a sense that we hear them and want to accommodate their needs and honor their communication preferences. And we should come to this from a genuine and authentic place, not by using tricks to manipulate the other person's impressions of us.

The other problem with the chameleon theory is that it provides a goal without the toolkit to achieve it. How do we know what to focus on when we're trying to be a chameleon? Simply speeding up or slowing down our pace in coordination with a customer is more awkward than helpful when establishing rapport.

DISC-EQ, then, is a far more valuable approach to use in our interactions with customers or business partners. The model removes the risk of mimicry while also providing us with the tools we need to read the styles of others and respond in effective and authentic ways, even when we've never met them before.

SEEING IT IN ACTION: ADJUSTING TO MY CUSTOMERS' STYLES

As a real estate sales professional, I love using DISC to connect with my clients. Being able to adapt my sales approach has undoubtedly increased my revenue. If I have a really people-focused I-style client, I show the hosting space and crowd-friendly amenities first. Likewise, if I have very systematic, analytical, and precise C-style client, I show the warran-

ties, efficiencies, and maintenance records before we even tour the property.

My DISC-EQ gives me the insight I need to read my customers and, more importantly, develop strategies on how to adapt my style to build more effective relationships.

ANDY, SALES REPRESENTATIVE

SHORT INTERACTIONS MAKE BIG DIFFERENCES

Although our focus in this book thus far has mostly been on building stronger long-term relationships with people we work with on a regular basis, we can't forget how crucial our interactions with those outside our circle are to our success.

After all, providing clients and business partners with meaningful interactions in which they feel truly heard can create enormous amounts of goodwill. At the same time, potential clients or partners are far more likely to choose our organization over another if they feel a strong connection with the company representatives they meet.

Building positive relationships outside our circle, then, can improve sales, increase customer retention, and strengthen collaboration. Ensuring positive outcomes to our short, less frequent interactions can be just as important as driving positive relationships within our daily work teams.

However, those shorter interactions present new challenges we haven't faced before in these pages. With clients and new colleagues, we may get only a single, brief window to establish the kind of positive rapport that leads to a fruitful, enduring relationship. Even when we speak with a person somewhat regularly, the brevity of these interactions can make forming a clear picture of their personality preferences a challenge.

SEEING IT IN ACTION: WE ARE ALL RESPONSIBLE FOR CUSTOMER SATISFACTION

My company manufactures products that are shipped around the United States, primarily via truck delivery. Because we value an aligned corporate culture, we have taught teams in every department to use DISC to improve how they interact with each other. But recently, those efforts yielded a wonderful and unexpected result.

After helping our truck drivers increase their DISC-EQ, the benefit of this common language stretched beyond the walls of our internal organization into the realm of our customers. Historically, our drivers' primary responsibility was to deliver shipments on time, with little emphasis on building quality relationships with the people receiving those shipments.

Since learning DISC, however, our drivers have started to put extra effort into their interaction with the customer. They've started to adjust their behaviors, and in turn, better relationships in the field have flourished.

Our drivers interact face-to-face with customers more than practically anyone else in our company. And since embracing DISC, they are receiving more customer compliments than ever before.

GRAYCE, MANAGER OF TALENT MANAGEMENT
AND CULTURE DEVELOPMENT

ARE YOU TRULY AWARE OF YOUR CUSTOMERS' NEEDS?

When working with customers or business partners, most of us realize that the onus is on us to make the relationship work. We are in a service-oriented role; our job is to understand our customers' needs and deliver solutions that solve those needs.

Most sales training includes guidance on how to complete a needs assessment and how to use *consultative selling* techniques—the selling approach that focuses on creating value and trust with a prospect by exploring their *business* needs before offering a solution. But what about your customers' *emotional* needs? After all, you are selling to human beings, and human beings have different DISC styles that lead to different emotional needs when having a conversation, including the one they are having with you.

Although DISC can't encapsulate the entirety of a person's emotional needs, it can provide some powerful insights that can be extremely helpful when trying to build a relationship with a customer or business partner.

As we've learned so far, we can predict that our D customers might have an emotional need to be productive and perhaps to feel in control of the conversation. I customers likely have an emotional need to feel connected with others in a positive and friendly way. S customers probably have an emotional need to feel supported and to be supportive of others. C customers might have an emotional need to have others recognize their competence.

The power of DISC is that it doesn't stop at just identifying these emotional needs. It also provides insight into communication-style preferences. For example, with your D customers, you'll know to err toward speaking more rapidly while also cutting to the chase. With I customers, you might speak just as quickly (likely matching their pace) while putting a little more emphasis on small talk and getting to know a bit about them personally. With S customers, you'll know to tone it down a bit while still putting effort into making the personal connection. And with your C customers, you'll keep that more measured pace while engaging them sooner in the details of the solutions you provide.

Going back to the "be a chameleon" strategy, DISC-EQ allows all the same tactics but with one very important difference: leveraging your DISC-EQ doesn't require you to be someone you aren't. You should never set aside your values, your morals, or who you really are. Customers will see right through that, and you'll get nowhere.

Applying your knowledge of DISC enables you to bring your authentic self. You can use these insights to guide how you adapt your behaviors to achieve better, more connected relationships. That is undoubtedly a straighter, more genuine route to success, both from a business perspective and a human one.

INSIGHTS: HOW WE INTERACT WITH CUSTOMERS

One thing we can absolutely say about ourselves: we love working with our customers and business partners. For years, we have been building deep, authentic human relationships with a lot of people whom we've had the pleasure to serve and work with. And those people certainly span the full spectrum of DISC styles.

We use our DISC-EQ to recognize the needs and preferences of the people we meet, and we apply that knowledge to form healthy and meaningful connections.

In practice, for Brett this can mean applying his self-awareness to know when he should unleash all his energy and enthusiasm and when he should rein it in a bit so as to not overwhelm the other person. For Evans, it can mean recognizing when to fully embrace his natural ability to be a great listener, allowing the other person to carry the conversation, and when he needs to step it up a bit to keep things moving.

Again, in no situation are we anything but authentic forms of ourselves. We just apply our understanding of DISC to know what parts of ourselves we should emphasize with any given person in any given interaction.

ESTIMATING OTHER PEOPLE'S STYLE

Finding the right balance in a conversation with someone new requires real flexing of your awareness of other styles in the moment of interaction. However, you aren't limited to relying on instinct alone to find the right balance. You can take the lessons from DISC-EQ and use them to connect with people in real time.

Think back to your mini-DISC assessment in chapter 3. By

considering two questions about pace and level of acceptance, you placed yourself in one of the four quadrants of the DISC wheel. If you are fast-paced and skeptical, the assessment would show you as a D. If you are fast-paced and more accepting, I would be your primary style. If you are more reserved and still accepting, you would be in the S quadrant. And if you are reserved and skeptical, your primary style is likely C.

Answering those questions for yourself was probably pretty easy. After all, you should know yourself pretty well. And assuming you've been working with your team for a while, you should have some insight into how to answer these questions for the people you work with most closely as well.

Answering these questions for someone you don't interact with regularly, though, can require a little more guesswork. However, you can still use this same observation-based process in your communication with customers and business partners. Be mindful during your interactions, especially with new individuals, and keep asking yourself: Is this person more fast-paced or more cautious? And, are they more skeptical or more accepting?

Within moments of saying hello, you can start to gauge where the person fits on the DISC wheel simply by being aware of how they speak, the kinds of questions they're asking, and their eagerness (or reticence) for small talk.

For example, if the person freely shares personal information, then you might assume they are closer to the accepting side, and thus an I or S. If they want to cut to the chase immediately and don't seem interested in any small talk, you might expect them to be more questioning and skeptical, and thus a D or a C.

In the same way, pay attention to their pace and energy to help you form a further determination of DISC style. Do they seem to move along quickly with high energy? Perhaps they are a D or I. Are they more reserved? Perhaps they are an S or C.

You can learn a lot about a person just by making a more conscious effort to pay attention to how they speak and act. Here are some general guidelines to help you further recognize the DISC style of the people you interact with:

- Ds tend to have a no-nonsense attitude, a straightforward or even blunt way of speaking, impatience with small talk, a quick and decisive style.
- Is tend to have an upbeat and enthusiastic attitude, friendly demeanor, interest in forming a personal relationship, willingness to try innovative ideas.
- Ss tend to have an agreeable and welcoming attitude, calm and gentle demeanor, frequent displays of modesty or accommodation, caution or hesitancy when making decisions.

- Cs tend to have a professional attitude, open skepticism, discomfort with small talk or personal questions, cautious when making decisions.

Once you have placed the person roughly in a DISC quadrant, you can make some basic assumptions about what they will value most during your interactions:

- Ds tend to value bottom-line results, competency, and quick action on the problems at hand.
- Is tend to value enthusiasm and excitement, a friendly and trusting relationship and quick action with immediate impact.
- Ss tend to value sincerity, a trusting relationship, dependability, and having time to consider their choices.
- Cs tend to value high-quality products and services, dependability, competency, and expertise and having time to do their own research and analyze their options.

A critical point for us to make: the ultimate goal here is not just to identify the person as a D, I, S, or C. A label on its own really serves no purpose and can do more harm than good if you aren't careful. Labeling a person after a single isolated interaction raises the risk of misunderstanding. For example, in any one-time situation, it would be entirely possible for an S-personality to come across as a D if they were in a hurry.

The value of this exercise is rooted in your ability to remain observant over time, and to use these insights to recognize how you should adjust your own behavior to be a more effective communicator, no matter who is on the other side of the conversation.

SEEING IT IN ACTION: PRESIDENTIAL APPRECIATION

I had just been elected to serve in a leadership role for our union, and I was invited to meet with the president of the college to discuss our new working relationship. Within minutes of my arrival, the president began asking me for a plan, for my intentions, for my strategy for engagement. The inquiries were coming fast. I started to see creeping frustration in her demeanor as I tried to align my thoughts.

Thankfully, I had worked with the president before in another situation. I recalled the time I saw her interacting with a technical project leader. The project leader was presenting an update to leadership, using a thirty-slide presentation chock-full of technical information. He didn't get through three slides before the president asked how any of this was relevant. After cutting him off a number of times, she impatiently left the meeting before he had finished the presentation.

I knew I didn't want our interaction to end like his did. So I sat up and said, "I understand you are a results-oriented, action person, probably a D on the DISC wheel. I have so much respect for your capabilities. However, I am a C-personality who weighs information and strives for accuracy in my answers. So if you will bear with me while I consider your questions, I believe I will be able to discuss all the issues and give you valuable feedback. Or, if you like, we can reschedule this meeting, and I will come back with answers to your questions."

I had no idea what would happen next. But I then witnessed a wonderful thing: appreciation. We went on to have a fruitful conversation and have had a great working relationship ever since.

MICHELLE, CHIEF INFORMATION OFFICER

THINK YOU AREN'T IN SALES? THINK AGAIN

At its core, the process of sales is simple: understand the needs of your audience, then convey how your ideas can help solve those needs. As such, it should be obvious that being a leader involves more than its fair share of selling. Whether you are convincing a client to use your products or services, trying to encourage a business partner to collaborate with you, or engaging a colleague in another department on the merits of a new project, you are always selling to someone. To quote author Daniel Pink,[22] "To sell is human," and doing it well is a central part of solving the people problem. If you want to see positive changes in your work environment, you must step forward, sell the value of your ideas, and get your colleagues to embrace your vision.

As we've seen time and again in this book, it's up to you to both live the change you want to see and to sell others on why they should follow your lead. The next—and final— chapter will help you do exactly that by applying the lessons of DISC-EQ directly to the behaviors that have been proven to drive leadership success.

APPLY IT YOURSELF: WORKING WITH THOSE OUTSIDE YOUR CIRCLE

It is crucial for you to be aware of the emotional needs and communication preferences of the people you are trying to serve, whether you are in a formal sales or customer service position or you are simply interacting with colleagues in or outside your organization. By anticipating those needs and preferences, you can adapt your speech and behavior to connect more quickly and more effectively with your

22 Daniel Pink, *To Sell Is Human: The Surprising Truth about Moving Others* (New York: Riverhead Books, 2012).

clients and partners, thus making it more likely that they will "hear you" as you explain how you can help solve their business needs.

D-Personalities
You're likely results-oriented and determined to ensure progress is achieved in every interaction. When working with those outside your immediate circle of colleagues, keep these strategies in mind:

- With Ds: They tend to value bottom-line results and quick action, so your styles will likely match well. They will appreciate your efforts to show how your product or service will help them achieve their goals.
- With Is: They tend to value friendly and trusting relationships, so you might want to spend a little extra effort on socializing and learning what is important to them personally. They share your focus on action, so get it done.
- With Ss: They tend to value friendly and trusting relationships, so try to connect on a personal level. Also, know that they might need a little extra time to consider the options, so don't get too aggressive in trying to close the deal.
- With Cs: They want to deal with competent people, so use your knowledge about your product or service to impress them. Before committing, they will want to see proof of dependability, so be prepared with your

facts. And be ready to slow your pace and give them time to decide.

I-Personalities

You are likely very enthusiastic and relationship-focused. When working with those outside your immediate circle of colleagues, keep these strategies in mind:

- With Ds: They tend to want to cut to the chase, so you'll probably want to pull back on the small talk. Make a quick connection, then move on to show you are focused on their goals, not yours. Be prepared to show proof that your product or service is as good as you say it is. They won't just take your word for it.
- With Is: They tend to value friendly relationships, so you should be able to connect on a personal level. Your conversations may be fun and lively, alternating between related and unrelated topics. Just don't get too caught up in small talk and forget to serve their business needs.
- With Ss: They tend to be polite and friendly, so you should be able to make that personal connection (as long as you stay sincere and don't get too overly energetic). Keep in mind that they may be hesitant to express concerns or objections, so be sure to ask what they are thinking.
- With Cs: They tend to be much more private than you, and sharing personal details may be uncomfortable

for them. As such, you'll likely want to stay focused mostly on business. They value details, so be ready to share relevant facts and data. Temper your energetic approach, and let the quality of your solution lead the way.

S-Personalities

You're very likely a great listener who cares deeply about how others feel about every topic you discuss. When working with those outside your immediate circle of colleagues, keep these strategies in mind:

- With Ds: They want to get to the bottom line quickly, so you might have to step up your pace a bit. Be prepared for their direct and perhaps blunt communication style. Don't be surprised when they ask some tough questions about how your product or service will help them reach their goals.
- With Is: They value trusting relationships, so your warm and friendly disposition should bode well. They like to move fast, so be ready to get your energy up before you make the call. If they really like and trust you, don't be shocked if they say yes sooner than you expect.
- With Ss: They tend to value sincerity like you, so go ahead and connect authentically. They will need time to make decisions, so stay engaged and be supportive.
- With Cs: They tend to be private, so hold back on the

personal sharing. They likely have done their home-work, so be sure to do yours. Come prepared with data and figures to support your claims, and be ready to answer some challenging questions.

C-Personalities

You're likely very detail-oriented and less focused on establishing strong relationships on a personal level. When working with those outside your immediate circle of colleagues, keep these strategies in mind:

- With Ds: They tend to value competency from their partners, so your focus on accuracy will be appreci-ated. They often don't need all the minute details, so hold back your more in-depth facts and figures until asked for them. D-personalities think and act quickly, so be ready to speed up your pace a bit.
- With Is: They tend to value enthusiasm and excite-ment, so muster up a little extra energy as you work with them. They are typically very social, which means engaging in small talk and sharing a little about your-self will likely strengthen your connection with them.
- With Ss: They tend to appreciate sincerity and friendli-ness, so presenting facts too soon may come across as cold or detached. They are accepting and aren't likely to challenge your data, but that doesn't mean they don't have concerns. Be sure to ask them.
- With Cs: They tend to value quality and accuracy, just

like you. Your logic and analytical approach will be appreciated. They will still need time to complete their own research, so be ready to provide additional details if needed.

Chapter 9

LEADERSHIP IS A RELATIONSHIP

MASTERING LEADERSHIP THROUGH DISC

Ken Guy is the director of the Finance and Business Operations Division at King County in Washington State. FBOD, as it's called, is the treasury department for the county and handles all of its financial management. Needless to say, Ken is the leader of a team that has huge responsibilities for his community. If Ken and his team don't do their jobs well, all of King County suffers.

For years, FBOD performed its role successfully, but new challenges arose, and there was a call for increasing performance levels to meet the county's needs. FBOD had many technically skilled people, but they did not always communicate or work together seamlessly.

Ken and the rest of his leadership team quickly found that they needed to adjust their culture if they were going to successfully improve communication and teamwork. To move FBOD forward, they would have to change how they led the organization. For Ken, this meant that he needed to develop his DISC-EQ and learn to lead in a new way.

Ken was very self-aware of his priorities and his limitations, but it turned out he wasn't as clear on how others perceived his personality. He thought of himself as reserved and reflective but also a friendly team player. He thought others saw him along those lines as well.

But going through a DISC workshop with his team, Ken found they did not always perceive his behavior in that light. Although, as an S, all of the priorities Ken saw in himself were indeed present, he was unaware that others misinterpreted his intentions. His team misread his cautiousness as a sign they shouldn't be looking to explore outside options or perspectives.

The discovery that others were reading his signals very differently than he intended was a wake-up call to Ken. As the leader, he would need to flex his DISC-EQ muscles and adjust how he came across to his immediate and more expansive circles so that he could better communicate his true intentions.

Crucially, he didn't change who he was; he simply changed his approach. He knew he had to communicate his commitment to the process by stepping outside his comfort zone, but that didn't mean he became an altogether different person; he just adapted how he communicated with his team. He would remain the same thoughtful, considerate S he had always been. He would just have to flex some of his less developed social muscles to create a more open environment that encouraged new ideas to flourish.

His opportunity came out of an attempt to improve one of his work processes. For months, FBOD had been working to drive higher levels of efficiency and effectiveness across the agency. As FBOD's leader, Ken was looking to accomplish process improvement just like the members of his staff. Part of his challenge was a strong culture of risk avoidance within the organization. He needed to inspire people to be willing to try things a little differently. With that goal in mind, Ken and his leaders were encouraging people to take small steps to incrementally streamline and improve how work got done.

However, as Ken and his team worked to address key inefficiencies across the office, they came to realize that the scope of their efforts was far too broad, and they had to discard their solutions up to that point. As an S, Ken didn't like to draw attention to himself, particularly his mistakes. So he promptly crumpled up the results of his early efforts and threw them away.

But then, he thought twice about that instinct and what it conveyed to those he worked with. He pulled the paper out of the trash, uncrumpled it, and taped it to his door with a note that read: "It's OK to fail."

Nothing could have communicated Ken's commitment to the change effort at FBOD more powerfully than that wrinkled piece of paper on the door of the head of the department. If the agency director was willing to experiment and learn, everyone in FBOD was empowered to do the same. They didn't have to be controlled by the fear of trying something that didn't work or experimenting and taking intelligent risks. They could strive to create a better way of working and working together. In fact, their new tagline became, "The best-run financial services for the best-run government in America." And thanks in part to Ken's willingness to *lead the way*, they are well *on their way* to solving the people problem.

SEEING IT IN ACTION: IT WAS LIKE READING MY DIARY

Part of my role is providing individualized DISC coaching for high-potential employees as they consider the jump into a management or executive role. One of the folks I worked with was an IT professional named Trina.

Trina had no familiarity with DISC and was skeptical of the assessment. I assured her that it would be painless, and we would interpret and discuss the results together. As I suspected, Trina manifested many of the C-style characteristics. She valued accurate work and had a high degree of conscientiousness.

As I went through the description of the C style, Trina told me she felt like I was reading her diary! She felt incredibly validated and for the first time excited about her potential new role. Prior to our meeting, Trina had decided to remove herself from consideration for a management position. Because of her discomfort with being the "up on stage" leader, she didn't think she could ever have a role of positional authority. However, as we talked through the value of the C style, I mentioned some well-known leaders who had the same style. We discussed some ways that her style was actually needed in leadership roles, par-

ticularly in her department, which needed a leader who could focus on details and ensure the job was done right.

DISC opened up a whole new world for Trina and also led to a more cohesive IT department when she was empowered to lead out of her natural style.

ABIGAIL, LEARNING AND DEVELOPMENT MANAGER

THE VALUE OF GOOD LEADERSHIP

FBOD has experienced tremendous success in large part because Ken understood the responsibilities of his position.

"People join organizations, and they leave their manager" is more than just an old saying; it's absolutely true. At the same time, we could also add, "People join organizations, and they *succeed* because of their leaders."

In their thirty-five-year study of leadership, Jim Kouzes and Barry Posner have proven that leaders directly affect how their teams feel about their responsibilities, their position, their potential, and their place in the organization. Kouzes and Posner have conducted ongoing research around the world with leaders from all walks of life. Their data proves that leaders who exhibit the Five Practices of Exemplary Leadership© more frequently have significant positive impacts on employee engagement and business results.

In their book, *The Leadership Challenge*, they share their research on what leaders do to create superior results:

- Model the Way
- Inspire a Shared Vision
- Challenge the Process
- Enable Others to Act
- Encourage the Heart

Each of these practices deal with how we communicate and work with the people we serve. DISC supports this model of leadership, helping leaders at all levels to perform each of these practices more successfully. In a way, the Five Practices tell you what a leader needs to *do*, whereas DISC shows you *how*.

For instance, we all know that a leader should provide an example of what they expect of others. This is the spirit of Model the Way, which highlights the importance of providing a consistent leadership vision that is authentic, yet adaptable enough to serve every member of the team. Your DISC-EQ can help inform how you adjust your communication to work with the people of various styles on your team while still being true to yourself and your leadership role.

Your DISC-EQ also helps you Inspire a Shared Vision more effectively by providing the means to recognize the emotional needs and communication preferences that different members of your team have, enabling you to craft and share your vision in a way that those needs and preferences are met.

When you want to Challenge the Process, your DISC-EQ gives you the tools to listen more attentively to different points of view and to open yourself to other perspectives. When you learn to honor other viewpoints, you are more likely to find innovative ways to improve how work gets done.

The more you understand about people's style traits and preferences, the better you'll be at equipping them with the skills and resources they need to get the job done. Once again, your DISC-EQ places the tools you need to Enable Others to Act right at your disposal.

When you want to Encourage the Heart of people you work with, you need to recognize and reward them in a way that truly honors who they are and what is important to them. Having a high DISC-EQ and understanding the motivators and stressors of different DISC styles could not be more valuable here.

While all of these strategies are reliant upon the others and indeed strengthen one another, there is a reason Kouzes and Posner place Model the Way first. The authentic self is so important to establishing trust and strong relationships that we must start there before we can implement the rest of the strategies. Thus, before we can Inspire, Challenge, Enable, and Encourage, we have to Model the Way forward for the whole team.

MODELING THE WAY

When team members see their leader developing cooperative relationships with the rest of the team, they perceive that leader to be more productive.[23] By publicly embracing your DISC-EQ, you can demonstrate to others how they can build more productive relationships.

When leaders act as good role models and develop authentic relationships, team members respond by becoming more productive, more engaged, and more integrated into the team. We should never underestimate the value of the leader's relationship with their team. When teammates struggle to accommodate each other's communication styles, a team can still function relatively effectively. It's not the most positive situation, but many teams can continue to get the job done even when friction is present among team members. However, when friction develops between a leader and members of the team, the ongoing disruption may be impossible to work around.

After all, it's from the leader that direct reports learn what is

23 Kouzes and Posner, *The Leadership Challenge*.

expected of them, how they are being measured, and if they are being successful. Perhaps most importantly, the leader communicates the model for how the team should interact and what it should prioritize. The smoother the relationship and the clearer the communication with a leader, the easier an individual or a team can achieve that success.

As a leader, it is your responsibility to create an environment in which everyone on your team can engage and work to the best of their abilities. It is your responsibility to Model the Way and show how you want others to behave.

You have to lead in creating strong working relationships with everybody on your team. You have to lead in recognizing where misunderstanding exists in your relationships and making improvements wherever you can. You have to lead in solving the people problem in all its forms so everyone can shine.

Luckily, by now, you know that having a high DISC-EQ will make you a much more effective and successful leader. Your DISC-EQ provides the insights you need to understand your own style traits, the tendencies and preferences of your fellow workers, and what is needed to make your colleagues feel comfortable and integrated within the team.

But awareness of these insights isn't enough. Like Ken, all leaders have to step up and demonstrate what those insights look like in action. A team can't be expected to nurture its relationships without the leader communicating that priority.

SEEING IT IN ACTION: LEARNING THE VALUE OF DIFFERENT STYLES

I've worked closely with Lisa for several years at the San Diego Humane Society, but our relationship changed when I took on a new leadership role that had several departments report to me, Lisa's included. I'm an ambitious and energetic leader, and when I took on this new role, I had many big changes in mind. But I also had concerns about how Lisa would take these changes. We have very different styles, and while I am an I who is eager to see change, Lisa is a more cautious S who might be reluctant to see her department evolve so quickly.

DISC provided us the means to work through what this transition, and my plans, meant to our relationship. Using my knowledge of Lisa and her DISC style, I decided to bring her into my process and share my thoughts with her before announcing the ideas to others. I utilized Lisa's patient, thoughtful nature to improve my communication and strengthen my ideas. This helped Lisa become more comfortable with the changes, and it helped me make sure I was meeting everyone's needs.

JERRICA, DIRECTOR OF STRATEGIC INITIATIVES

SERVICE BEFORE POWER

Throughout this book, we have been careful in choosing our words when discussing hierarchy within organizations. We should know by now how easy it is to dismiss others with unintentional miscommunication when using careless language. When we talk about those in positions "below" us or being in a position "over" another, we may unintentionally communicate that the needs of our fellow workers are less worthy of concern than our own. When we speak in terms of "above" and "below," "higher" and "lower," and "under" and "over," we express ourselves in dynamics of power. Good leadership inevitably wrestles with questions of power, but we should consider it introspectively. We should each ask ourselves, "What is the purpose of the power that has been place in my hands as a leader of this team, department, or organization?"

This may seem like a very philosophical question for such a practical book, but your answer has real bearing on how successfully you can implement the lessons of DISC for yourself and across your team.

If you see your leadership role primarily through the lens of authority, you may be tempted to build your relationships with an "above-below" hierarchy. You may come to expect others to adapt to you and your style characteristics. And you may see success in terms of personal advancement *over* team achievement.

On the other hand, if you approach your leadership position from a perspective of service, you'll be more inclined to look for ways to accommodate others so that the team *and* the individuals on it all succeed together.

Seeing leadership as service, then, allows you to benefit everyone, yourself included. And you can develop that service mentality by increasing your awareness of how your leadership affects others on your team and within your organization.

As leaders, we should see ourselves as in service to what the whole team is trying to accomplish for our organization. To achieve our goals, we must support the people we work with because their success is the organization's success, which ultimately is also our success. And the people on our team succeed when we are able to meet their needs.

If we approach our position with that attitude, then it makes perfect sense for us to Model the Way in stretching beyond our comfort zone and finding better ways to decide, communicate, and handle conflict. We understand the need to flex first instead of expecting others to flex for us.

According to this definition of leadership, you must go beyond being a manager and also be a coach. Managers set direction, measure performance, and perform other management duties, all of which are important for organizational success. But coaches go further. Coaches help others grow by equipping them with the tools, resources, and insights they need to do their best work.

If you subscribe to this service-oriented philosophy, then increasing your DISC-EQ is an invaluable step to take. It allows you to understand how you and your direct reports are interacting, how they see you, how you can create a motivating environment, and what you can do to enable them to do their best.

HOW YOUR STYLE INFLUENCES YOUR LEADERSHIP

Leaders come from every DISC style, and good leaders understand how their style influences how they lead others. To become the best leader you can be, you have to raise your awareness of your own style and how that style might influence how you lead.

Once you have moved into a position of authority, your influence with others vastly increases; it becomes ever more important to understand the impact of your actions. If you are a D, you may have previously found success as an individual contributor by pushing your points strongly and driving to clear the items off your list as quickly as possible. As a leader, your forcefulness may put additional pressure on the team reporting to you.

Likewise, if you are a C, you may find that the skepticism and analysis that allowed you to effectively improve workflows now feels critical from the position of leadership. As an S who supported the team outside the meeting room, you may need to step forward and be more decisive as the person showing the way forward for the whole group. Finally, if you are an I whose enthusiasm inspired others as a team member, you may find that the same pace adds stress and tension when setting the standards for all.

As a leader, you need to think more about the impact your natural style has on others with whom you are working. By increasing your DISC-EQ, you'll be in a good position to do that effectively, enabling you to leverage the best of your traits while also ensuring that you consider the needs and preferences of others.

LEADERS KNOW EVERYONE'S STYLE

Being an authentic leader means you need to be you, but you also need to be able to adapt to meet the style needs of everyone on your team. So even though becoming aware of your style and how that affects your leadership and relationships is important, you must also invest time in expanding your knowledge of the DISC styles of everyone on your team. If you have five members on your team, you have to be able to understand the priority needs and communication preferences for each of those five members. You have to be able to live within an authentic leadership style while also adapting your behaviors to bring the best out of each team member.

In fact, just by knowing the DISC styles on your team, you can make some immediate leadership adjustments. You can begin to institute things such as:

- With Ds: Provide clear goals and allow them to make decisions about how to meet the targets.
- With Is: Embrace their enthusiasm and give them opportunities to work closely with others.
- With Ss: Give them time to get comfortable with new ideas and encourage them to share their thoughts.
- With Cs: Share the logic behind your requests and allow them time to gather their thoughts.

Although you want to have a single leadership philosophy that brings the team together, you need to develop different strategies that make your philosophy work for the individual members of the team. Once you know the DISC priorities of all your team members, you can tailor your communication with each of them to be as effective as possible.

REWARDS AND RECOGNITION

One of the places where a misreading of styles is most apparent is when we Encourage the Heart with rewards and recognition. Often, we put very little thought into *how* to reward our supporting team. We assume rewards of any kind are always welcome. However, although almost everyone does appreciate recognition and praise of one sort or another, the form of that recognition is key to ensuring a reward is seen as a reward and not a punishment.

Some on your team, such as those with D or I styles, may appreciate being brought up in front of the rest of the team for public recognition. For others, such an experience can be stress-inducing and unpleasant. A C-personality, for instance, may stress over saying exactly the right thing when in front of others. An S-personality may feel awkward being singled out.

A good leader, then, should take their knowledge of DISC and develop rewards that suit each member of the team. A private word of appreciation from you may mean far more than the chance to shine in front of colleagues. You can only know how to deliver a reward when you know the person's personal preferences and underlying emotional needs.

Evans learned this lesson the hard way. Early in his career in management, he took it upon himself to reward one of his direct reports with the opportunity to present the team's work to the senior executive committee.

He intended this as a sign of great confidence in her skills and recognition of her contribution to the project, but he hadn't taken her fear of public speaking into account. She preferred to work quietly far away from the spotlight. Evans meant this opportunity to be an honor, but for her, it was a nightmare.

When he delivered the news, she burst into tears, catching Evans by surprise. They talked through the situation and decided to remove her from the speaking role, instead finding another approach for recognizing her efforts that she found more invigorating. He learned that day how important it is to reward team members by first considering what type of recognition would be appreciated from their perspective.

As a leader, you can't help your team be as successful as possible unless you understand how to recognize them and show appreciation effectively.

Consider these potential forms of recognition when next rewarding someone on your team:

- With Ds: Acknowledge their accomplishments and let them take on bigger challenges.
- With Is: Provide public recognition both for their achievements and their ideas.

- With Ss: Avoid public fanfare and show your appreciation in private.
- With Cs: Praise them privately and call out details of their contributions that you most appreciate.

LEADERS HAVE TO BRING IT ALL TOGETHER

The role of leadership is not easy in any organization. A successful leader has to do more than just become an expert in their specialized field; they have to engage with everyone from a place of empathy and high emotional intelligence.

To that end, good leaders can't just dabble in DISC-EQ; they have to thoroughly implement the framework across all their relationships. The modern, team-focused environment requires you to open yourself to all the insights that DISC-EQ has to offer you about your decision-making, communication inside and outside the team, conflict resolution, and leadership because you have to set the standards for everyone else.

You set the tone, inspire with your vision, challenge the status quo, and enable others to do their best and rise. Therefore, it's up to you to expand your DISC-EQ so that you can live up to your highest leadership potential.

APPLY IT YOURSELF: LEADERSHIP

Leaders usually have a wider span of influence than individual contributors. They tend to interact with more people and have a larger impact on many in their organization. To be the best leader you can be, it's helpful to stay mindful of what excites you and what drains you. Use the ideas below to help you balance your workload, plan your schedule, and keep your energy up, for your own benefit and for the benefit of everyone around you.

D-Personalities

What you may find most enjoyable about leading people:

- Setting ambitious goals for your team
- Being able to implement your own ideas
- Making important decisions
- Achieving superior results with your team

Aspects of leadership that you may not enjoy as much:

- Being patient while you listen to the opinions of others
- Working within a bureaucracy you feel is unnecessary and inefficient
- Engaging in small talk when there is work to be done
- Revisiting topics when people do not pick up on ideas as quickly as you would like

I-Personalities

What you may find most enjoyable about leading people:

- Inspiring people to rise to challenges
- Building strong, positive relationships with your colleagues
- Getting people excited and enthused about the team's mission and goals
- Celebrating success with your team

Aspects of leadership that you may not enjoy as much:

- Engaging in difficult conversations that may be emotionally unpleasant
- Performing structured, repetitive tasks that leave no room for creativity
- Slowing your pace to focus on details
- Having to closely monitor the performance of others

S-Personalities

What you may find most enjoyable about leading people:

- Creating an environment where people genuinely care about each other
- Coaching a team to work together toward a common goal
- Listening and supporting people when they face challenges
- Complimenting people and sharing credit for a job well done

Aspects of leadership that you may not enjoy as much:

- Standing your ground when things get tense and people get emotional
- Providing corrective feedback or discipline, especially when you anticipate pushback
- Taking risks that will upset people or make them uncomfortable
- Dealing with a chaotic workplace

C-Personalities

What you may find most enjoyable about leading people:

- Building a systematic approach that delivers consistent results
- Catching and correcting flaws in logic, rationale or process design
- Ensuring that you and your team produce to the highest standards
- Using analysis to solve complex business challenges

Aspects of leadership that you may not enjoy as much:

- Being pushed to make decisions before you have all the data you'd like
- Dealing with people that do not meet your standards of performance
- Being challenged about your approach or analysis
- Celebrating publicly with your team

CONCLUSION

Relationships can be challenging, even when they are built on honesty and openness. In this book, we've seen gifted leaders across numerous industries struggle to create healthy work environments in which everyone can thrive. The people problem plagues teams of all shapes and sizes, across industries as diverse as medicine, technology, government, animal welfare, and finance.

We now know that dysfunction doesn't have to be a part of our work relationships. When we are willing to take the lead, open ourselves to introspection and to the insights of DISC, and then take action, we can remove the personality friction that makes issues and problems more difficult to address. Throughout these pages, we've seen leaders create successful, positive relationships between individuals and across whole organizations. And they've done it, every time, by building up their DISC-EQ.

DISC-EQ is at the heart of successful leadership because it provides a framework through which we can understand one another and address differences through concrete action. It provides us the language to discuss our different perspectives and a path to bridging misunderstanding.

Each chapter in this book expresses a crucial aspect of your role as a leader and how you can choose your actions wisely and adapt your behavior for the mutual benefit of all. Successful leadership is built on successful relationships, and those relationships will be on firmer footing when you apply your DISC-EQ with a consistent commitment to honesty, vulnerability, and trustworthiness.

Although the focus of this book has been on building work relationships that work, the power of DISC-EQ doesn't stop at the office door. This framework can help strengthen your empathy and thoughtfulness and provide you with meaningful guidance in all your relationships. So keep these ideas in mind as you interact with spouses, children, parents, friends, acquaintances, and even strangers.

Although we tried to pack in as much value as possible in this book, we have really scratched only the surface of DISC-EQ. To truly optimize your relationships and upgrade your emotional intelligence, we encourage you to visit SolvingThePeopleProblem.com and make use of the resources available. There, you will not only find the

DISC-EQ Survey we mentioned in chapter 2 but also articles, assessments, and tools to guide you and help you make the most of these ideas. With just ten or fifteen minutes of your time, you could soon have a far deeper appreciation of how you are approaching life and work and how others are perceiving that approach. While you are there, please reach out to us directly and share your stories and questions. We'd love to be active participants in your DISC-EQ journey.

Investing in our relationships and ourselves is a lifelong pursuit. So whenever you are ready to solve the people problem in your workplace—or anywhere else in your life—we will be here to help.

Brett Evans

ACKNOWLEDGMENTS

This book would not have become a reality without input and support from a great many people. At the risk of sounding like an Academy Awards acceptance speech, we wish to thank the following people and teams:

Our wonderful wives, Joan and Maxine. Thank you both for all your love and support.

The fantastic team that has made Integris Performance Advisors such a success over these years: Samantha Kerrigan, Gwen Voelpel, Dan Schwab, Amy Dunn, Colleen Kindler, Ed Vasko, Mason Chock, Tolu Perales, Holly Allen, Amy Leneker, Robin Kellogg, Renee Harness, Tom Pearce, Mark Welch, Dick Heller, Althea Saldanha, Karlo Tanjuakio, KJ Jenison, and of course, Tracy O'Rourke.

The people who graciously shared their stories and insights

about how DISC-EQ has helped them build work relationships that really work: Ken Guy, Lisa Murphy, Chauntelle Hellner, Jerrica Owen, Gary Weitzman, Eunjoo Greenhouse, Kimberly Kochurka Shaw, Carmel Call, Caroline Whalen, Reid Swanson, Sarah Richardson, Stephanie Nater, Kendall Mealy, Grayce Langheine, Michelle Tuscher, Megan Roy, Nancy Williams, Abigail Nishimoto, Brian Daugherty, Katherine Shenar, Nathan Meyer, Darrell Damron, Lana Stuart-Eskeli, Jana Hawkins, Michelle Doherty, Lisa Boelkes, Lori Kasma, Tina Nguyen, Natalie Loeb, Kelsey Anderson, Andy Widen, Jason Ingram, Cassandra Muehe, and Hannah Aoyagi.

Our business partners, without whom we couldn't offer the world-class services we do: Cherryl D'Souza, Katie Fuhrman, Romain Mallard, Susie Kukkonen, Mark Scullard, Jidana James, Clare McInerney, Beth Dentinger Keup, Rebecca Halat, Craig Meiners, Jeremy Stewart, Julie Straw, Val Anderson, Abby Field, Elise Bixby, Desiree Skowronek, Tim Schwanz, Rachel Vliem, Amanda Balgaard, Shirley Norgren, and Barry Davis.

The other experts from whom we continue to learn (and reference in this book): Barry Posner, Jim Kouzes, Patrick Lencioni, Travis Bradberry, Jean Greaves, Simon Sinek, Brené Brown, Susan Cain, Daniel Goleman, and Daniel Pink.

Our publishing team who had to put up with us as we worked on this project: Seth Libby, Bailey Hayes, Zach Obront, Cindy Curtis, Josh Raymer, and Tucker Max.

The fabulous people at our deeply valued clients whom we've had the honor to serve: King County (with special shout-outs to DES, FBOD, ORMS, BRC, WTD, and RALS), SoCalGas, San Diego Gas and Electric, Cedars Sinai, Blue Cross Blue Shield of Louisiana, Oracle, Salesforce, San Diego Humane Society, Optum, ICW Group, Comcast, Turkey Hill Dairy, the county of Santa Cruz, the county of Los Angeles, Centegra Health System, Commonwealth Care Alliance, PAEA, the city of SeaTac, the city of Shoreline, Snohomish County, DCAMM, the University of Southern California, AZ State (with special callouts to the Government Transformation Office and the Departments of Revenue, Corrections, and Health Services), Trustmark Insurance, Radian Guaranty, ADP, Milliman, Sacramento Sewer, TaxAudit, Chair Academy, Sempra Energy, Hasbro, The Association for Animal Welfare Advancement, ECFMG, CAMC Health Systems, SUPERCHARGED Companies, Defense Intelligence Agency, Alaska Commission on Postsecondary Education, the county of Kauai, and the state of Washington (with special shout-outs to Results Washington and the Departments of Licensing, Enterprise Services, and Ecology).

ABOUT THE AUTHORS

BRETT M. COOPER and **EVANS KERRIGAN** help professionals like you build work relationships that really work. Over the last twenty years, they've influenced thousands of people in government, nonprofits, and corporate America to work together in more productive, more effective, and more human ways.

Through Integris Performance Advisors—the firm they co-founded—Brett and Evans have helped clients increase employee engagement, improve efficiency, and generate hundreds of millions in financial benefit.

Brett and Evans are frequent speakers on team dynamics, leadership, and operational excellence. To access more great content and resources and to connect directly with Brett and Evans, visit SolvingThePeopleProblem.com.

Made in the USA
Coppell, TX
03 October 2020